D1100432

THE
GARDENERS' WORLD
COTTAGE GARDEN

In the same series

Gardeners' World Vegetable Book

THE
GARDENERS' WORLD
COTTAGE GARDEN

GEOFF HAMILTON

DRAWINGS BY
LORNA TURPIN

BRITISH BROADCASTING CORPORATION

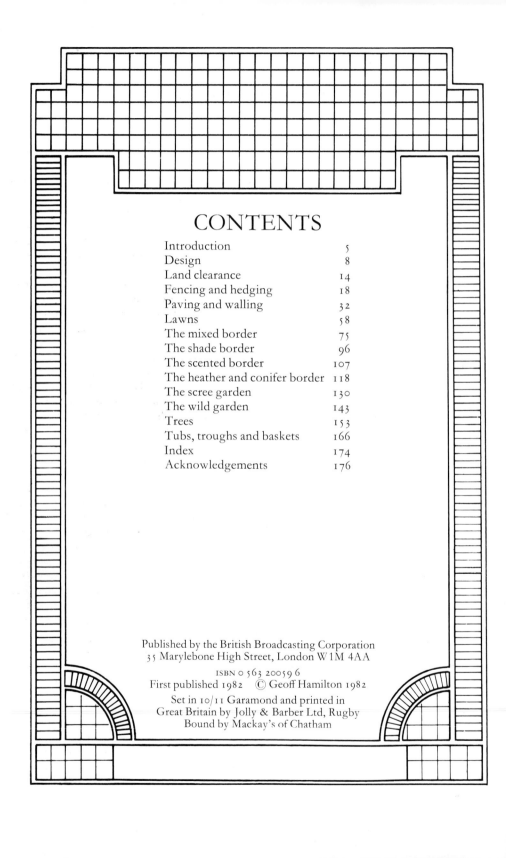

CONTENTS

Published by the British Broadcasting Corporation
35 Marylebone High Street, London W1M 4AA

ISBN 0 563 20059 6
First published 1982   © Geoff Hamilton 1982

Set in 10/11 Garamond and printed in
Great Britain by Jolly & Barber Ltd, Rugby
Bound by Mackay's of Chatham

INTRODUCTION

Making a garden is a creative art that we *all* have the talent for. Unlike most other fields of art no special gift is required, no great manual dexterity nor 'special' sensitivity. Even the clumsiest of philistines can make a good garden.

That is not to say that there have not been great garden artists; there have been, and still are, a few gifted people who can visualise and build a garden that is a source of pleasure to all. But the art of gardening is an essentially *personal* thing. It's the classic example of art for the artist.

It is you who has to live with your garden, so you should create it just for yourself. For this reason, of course, there is a limitless variation in garden design. What may be perfect for you, may turn the stomach of the next-door neighbour. But that doesn't matter a bit. If you like it, do it! You can rest assured that, however inept you may think you are at the start, Nature will lend a hand to turn your creation into a thing of beauty.

I shall limit myself to describing how I created the cottage garden at Barnsdale, in the hope that it may give you some ideas for your own garden. What I think is more important, is to describe the practical techniques that will enable you to turn your ideas into realities.

Having said that, it is obvious that there are some, basic design rules that should be noted even if they are not all adhered to. It may be clear that curved borders will give greater flexibility of planting, but it is not so obvious that wide paths actually increase the sense of space in the garden, even though they take up more room. So I have indulged myself by suggesting a few basic design rules that have been applied to the Barnsdale garden. After those, you're on your own.

One thing I think I should explain right at the beginning is that although I believe that the old 'cottage garden' *principles* are best for small modern gardens, some variations are necessary.

Architecture has changed, plant varieties and forms have evolved, materials have developed and present day requirements for the garden have altered considerably. Certainly many of the ideas we have been following for the last hundred years must go. Many of those basic principles were developed by the architects and designers of the 'great' gardens of England. We no longer have the room to even contemplate the massive herbaceous borders, rose gardens or shrubberies of that bygone era. We must cut our coats according to the cloth, and tailor our designs to suit the space available. So, we must think in terms of mixed planting, of using smaller trees and shrubs and of making the best of the more modern materials that we can afford.

We must also carefully consider the enormous changes that have taken place in the design of our houses. Few of us are lucky enough to live in either a stately home or a pretty little thatched cottage that cries out for roses round the door. We are much more likely to have settled for a square semi on a modern housing estate. Far from being limiting, the simplicity of modern architecture provides exciting possibilities and an irresistible challenge to the keen gardener. The barest wall can be transformed with climbing plants, and the starkest lines can be softened with imaginative planting. Even the tiniest plot in the middle of a vast urban sprawl can become an oasis of colour, interest and beauty.

My little cottage at Barnsdale is, I suppose, something between the modern estate house and a rural country cottage. Built just under a hundred years ago as two farm cottages, the design is nothing short of utilitarian. A simple, rectangular 'box' relieved only by a rather attractive gabled roof.

When I moved in, the garden had been neglected for several years. It was easy to lose oneself in the jungle of weeds. It was quite obvious that I would have to start from scratch and that the task would be by no means plain sailing. The challenge was there and it was with eagerness that I picked up the glove.

Geoff Hamilton,
Barnsdale, 1982

Above right: at first sight, the cottage garden looked a daunting prospect. Head-high in weeds and brambles it was obviously going to be no easy job. But, with the help of a hefty dose of weedkiller and a bit of machinery, it soon began to take shape

Right: only eighteen months later, it begins to look like a real garden. The lawn is well established, and the borders are made colourful with annuals until the shrubs and herbaceous plants fill out

DESIGN

Perhaps the most difficult task for a gardener with a new plot to 'tame', is to curb his enthusiasm. I know that when I first laid eyes on what was to be my new garden at Barnsdale, I could hardly resist the urge to rush out and hack away at the weeds. That would have been a big mistake.

Before pulling a weed, or turning a spade of soil, it is *essential* to think long and hard, make copious notes, and commit your ideas to paper. Attacking the task piecemeal, with no preordained plan in mind will never result in a cohesive layout. The garden must be planned as a whole, even if the final completion takes several years.

Concept

I apologise for the word 'concept'. But don't worry, I'm not about to launch into an airy-fairy abstract dissertation on the philosophy of gardening. Far from it. But it is important to decide right at the outset, what you expect from your garden, and how best you can achieve it.

I'm one of those awkward gardeners who want a bit of everything. A nightmare to the professional designer, especially if the garden is on the small side. No 'theme gardens' for me; no 'tonal borders' of one monotonous colour. I am an inveterate plant enthusiast, and I want to grow them *all*. And that's where my 'cottage garden' concept comes in.

Now, I wouldn't like to suggest that this is the sort of cottage garden the Victorians were so fond of; nor does it really resemble the jumble of flowers and herbs in the original country cottage gardens. But many of its features are similar.

First of all, the garden is small. Most gardens are these days, so I feel that the Barnsdale concept should fit most modern gardens very well. The limitation of size does present some special problems which cannot be solved by sticking to the rule-book of the nineteenth and early twentieth-century designers. It needs an entirely new approach.

It would be folly, however, to completely disregard all the lessons that were learned from those great gardeners who had acres and acres to play with. Their ideas were good, but unfortunately our canvas is considerably smaller.

A perfect example was my dilemma over the 'rose garden'. Much as I love roses, I realised at a very early stage, that I simply didn't have the room for a formal rose garden. But I love those rectangular beds set in grass with just one variety to each bed. That way, all the roses bloom at the same time in each bed, all are at the same height and all the same colour. The result is a striking, mass display. So, I broke the rules and planted my roses in the mixed border – not singly, scattered here and there as the original cottage gardeners may have done, but all together in a block. By using one variety only in the block, I have achieved that same mass display I would have had in a formal rose garden, but in much less space.

Mind you, I am not averse to planting the odd rose here and there for a special reason. When I found a variety with a really outstanding perfume, for example, I had to have just one bush in my little perfumed corner. But there, of course, I was not looking for mass display.

I am also much influenced by other peoples' ideas. I suppose most of us are. In the course of my job, I travel around a lot of gardens, nurseries and flower shows. I am continually seeing ideas that would adapt well to fit the scheme at Barnsdale. A good example was Adrian Bloom's heather and conifer garden which I first saw at the Chelsea Flower Show. It looked so attractive that I felt it would make a fine feature at Barnsdale. However, I did adapt it a little, by growing several other species of acid-loving plants apart from heathers. The flowers and foliage of dwarf rhododendrons and azaleas and the bright berries of gaultheria add a deal of interest for me. I even have the odd few snowdrops peeping through in the early spring. There again you see, that is almost certainly not what the original designer had in mind. Yet it suits me and my garden very well.

Essentials

So, the main concept of my garden is that it should provide a home and a setting for plants – lots and lots of plants. The next step is to consider the essentials.

In every garden there are certain things that must be provided for and often a few problems to solve as well. For example, most gardens need a dustbin and a clothes line. If you have children, they'll need somewhere to play, or, if you're a sun-lover you'll need a sunny spot to lie out in. These essentials must be noted and planned for right at the start.

At Barnsdale, the item at the top of the list was the view. On two sides, it is magnificent. From my vantage point on the top of the hill, I look over a vast expanse of water to the rolling countryside beyond. That view had to be retained. On the third side there is a small wood, but the view from the remaining boundary is not so good. Here, my friend the local car repairer works on the most motley collection of old bangers it has ever been my misfortune to see. They have to be hidden.

The only other problem at Barnsdale is the wind. Living on the top of a hill does have its problems. Whichever direction it blows, we get it – the full force. Wind, apart from being uncomfortable, can have a serious effect on plants, particularly when

The basic plan, Barnsdale
The basic plan must be fairly
flexible. At this stage, only
the broad planting areas are
outlined.

1   The house
2   Outhouse
3   Barn
4   Lawn
5   Paving planted with alpines
6   Scree garden
7   Brick circle
8   Stone urn
9   Paving
10 Stepping stones
11 Stepping stones set in gravel
    with alpines between
12 Steps
13 Fence
14 Table and seats
15 Dwarf wall
16 Post and rail fencing
17 Hedge
18 Low hedge
19 Woodland
20 Rough grass
21 Rough grass planted with
    shrubs
22 New tree planting to link
    with woodland
23 Feature tree
24 Tall screen trees and shrubs
25 Existing Ash underplanted
    with shade-loving plants
26 Mixed border
27 Shade border
28 Scented border
29 Fern border
30 Roses
31 Heather and conifer border
32 Annuals

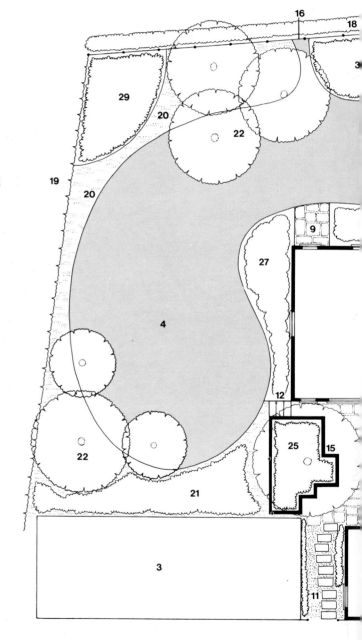

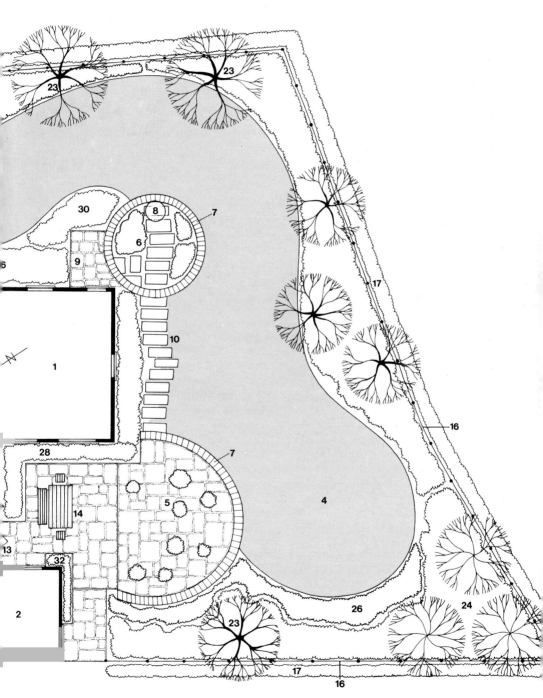

they are young. It tends to evaporate water from the leaves at an alarming rate and, if the roots can't replace it quickly enough, cells in the leaves die off and leaf scorch occurs. On some plants, like conifers, this has a very disfiguring and alas, a lasting effect.

So, a windbreak-cum-screen was one of my essentials. On the 'ugly' side it could be a tall, continuous hedge, while on the remaining two windy sides, the planting would have to be more judicious in order to retain the view.

The garden is also blessed with a sun-trap. Since this is adjacent to the back-door, it cries out for a paved area where I can eat my meals on sunny days. That is, in my opinion, one of the civilised luxuries of life.

Finally, it is important to consider the amount of time you have to maintain your garden. It's not a bit of good working out an elaborate design if you will be forced to neglect it. Don't get me wrong now. I love my gardening, but with two acres of trials ground to look after as well – apart from all my other 'duties' – I just don't have the time to fiddle about. So, the lawn area was designed in long, sweeping curves to eliminate awkward mowing and edge cutting.

The planting is dense and informal with lots of ground-cover to cut down the chore of weeding, and I have deliberately avoided features which require a lot of maintenance. For example, though I love alpine plants, I decided that a rock garden was simply not on. I don't have the space to do the job properly but, more important, I simply haven't the time for a rock garden's high labour requirement. So, I compromised by settling for a scree garden. That way, I can still have my alpines, but without all that work, weeding out intruders from tiny crevices in the rocks. But more of that later.

The plan

Before starting to plan the garden on paper it's necessary to have an accurate drawing of the site. So, a few basic surveying techniques will have to be employed. You don't need to be an Einstein to do it and all you need is a surveyor's long tape.

Start by drawing a very rough plan. Then select a couple of fixed points in the garden. The corners of the house are the obvious ones to use.

To fix exactly the first corner of the garden, measure from both house corners, and mark the measurements on the rough drawing. Then repeat the process for the other three corners. Also, at this stage, measure the lengths of the boundaries and the exact measurements of the house.

When it comes to drawing up the masterplan more accurately, start by drawing in the house. Then measure from the corners of the house to the corners of the garden and draw a couple of arcs. Where the lines cross, will be the exact position of the first

My little sun-trap corner simply had to be paved. Eventually, the plants will grow to soften the hard lines

1 Measure the distances A & B from both corners of the house to the corner of the garden

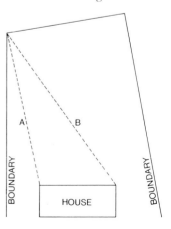

2 On the drawing, mark two arcs. The point where they cross is the corner of the garden

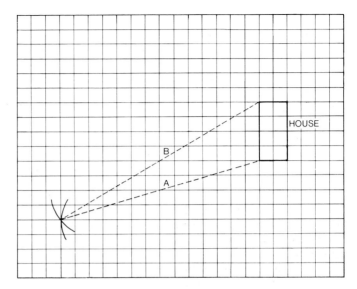

HOUSE

B

A

corner. Repeat the process with the second corner and join the two with a line to show the boundary. Check the length on the plan with the length you measured just to make sure, and then draw in the other boundaries in the same way. If you have any other fixed points, like a tree you don't want to remove, for example, measure and mark them on the plan in the same way.

When you have drawn the masterplan, pin it to a board and cover it with a piece of tracing paper. You'll change your mind a lot during the design stage, and this saves defacing the masterplan. It's worth while taking a lot of time over the design. When I was working on the plan for the Barnsdale garden, I spent a couple of weeks and at least three pads of tracing paper. And even when you have the scheme more or less as you want it, you must still be prepared to be flexible. On paper, what you see is a bird's-eye view. When the plan is transformed to the ground, the lines are seen from another perspective entirely. What may look like a good line on paper, may look quite wrong on the land. If it does, change it. Remember that, since the idea is to make a design that is pleasing to the eye, the golden rule is that if it looks right, it *is* right.

LAND CLEARANCE

Start a garden on dirty land, and you'll be in trouble for the rest of your life. There's no doubt about it, it pays hands down to get rid of all the weeds and rubbish completely, right at the start. Otherwise you'll be battling against weeds forever, and so will your plants. This is particularly important, of course, if the ground is infested with pernicious perennial weeds like couch grass, ground elder or oxalis. These days, thank goodness it's not a difficult task.

The garden at Barnsdale contained every type of weed known to man: ground elder, couch, nettle, thistles, bindweed, brambles – they were all there in their thousands and all thriving. And that is just the time to attack. When they are growing well and they have plenty of foliage, they will absorb a translocated herbicide – one that goes through the leaves to the roots – like a hungry schoolboy locked in the tuck shop. So, the very first job was to spray the whole garden with a weedkiller containing glyphosate. Murphy make one called 'Tumbleweed'.

The plants absorb the weedkiller through their leaves and take it down to the root system. There it has the effect of preventing the roots from storing food. So, after a while, the plant will die. Obviously it takes time for the weedkiller to take effect, so it is important to give it a chance to get down to the roots before cultivating the soil or stripping off the tops of the weeds.

When the material is applied, it is much more effective if it is sprayed on rather than applied through a watering can. Even with a sprayer, it is, surprisingly, more effective to put on too little than too much. The idea is to try to get the liquid to stay on the leaves in tiny drops. Once it starts running off, less spray stays on the leaf and therefore less is absorbed. There is absolutely no advantage in soaking the weeds thoroughly. Anyway, it's none too cheap, so it's worth being a bit miserly.

There is one group of weeds that is fairly resistant even to glyphosate. Any that have shiny, glossy leaves tend to shed the weedkiller before there is a chance to absorb it. Weeds like marestail and oxalis will do this – and there was plenty of both at Barnsdale. With these it is necessary to break through that waxy coating. I did it with a besom broom. Fortunately, I don't have any close neighbours or they may have thought I had finally tipped over the edge. I simply went round the garden uttering loud oaths at the infamous villains, and slashing at them with the broom. This effectively bruised the leaf surfaces and allowed the weed-killer to enter.

After a couple of weeks, the weeds showed signs of discolouring and wilting. The time had come to get rid of them completely.

Here, I have to admit, I cheated. I did make a brave attempt to plough the dead weeds in with a big rotavator, but there was simply too much top growth. It was impossible to bury and simply clogged up the tines. Anyway, the beginning of the growing season was creeping up fast, and I wanted to get on.

So I called in a gigantic mechanical digger and a large lorry. I've found that the operators of these machines are generally pretty expert, and fortunately, my man was no exception. He managed to skim off the weeds with no more than about half-an-inch of topsoil. The whole lot was dumped in the lorry and carted away.

I wasn't sorry to see the back of them, I can tell you. The machine then roughly graded the land to the contours I wanted and he even pulled out a couple of old concrete fence posts.

The best machine for the job is called a Drott, and it's worth asking for one with a 'four-in-one' bucket. This is an ingenious device that is hinged in several places. It can be used like an ordinary shovel, or it can open up like the mouth of some great fiery monster, to pull out unwanted tree stumps, boulders, posts or anything else that's in the way. The whole operation took a day, and it cost me £70. I reckon it was money well spent.

A large cultivator can be hired quite cheaply, and will save a tremendous amount of work when preparing the lawn. Borders are best cultivated more deeply

But even then I wasn't satisfied with my weed-killing job. The growth had been so thick, that I was worried that some weeds had escaped and their roots were left in the ground. I therefore allowed them to regrow. They did, in a remarkably short time. Then I sprayed them again, and so far, I have had little trouble, except for one persistent patch of bindweed and I'll tell you later how I finally beat that.

The soil at Barnsdale is very light and sandy, so water is lost very quickly. If this happens the plant nutrients go with it, so I felt that it would be a wise precaution to improve the water-retention of the soil before sowing seed and planting plants.

Organic matter was called for in large quantities. In fact, unless the soil is organic itself, like the beautiful black Fenland soils of East Anglia, it always pays to dig in organic matter underneath lawns and permanent borders. It seems contradictory but as well as improving the water retention of light soils this will also assist drainage on heavy clays. On a sticky soil the organic matter breaks it up to allow water to pass through, while in light land, water is held within the organic matter itself.

1 Areas to be turfed can generally be single dug or rotavated

2 Mark out the lawn area with canes, since this needs only relatively shallow cultivation

Because I have a cheap and plentiful source, I always use well-rotted farmyard manure at Barnsdale. If this were not the case, I would plump first for spent mushroom compost, spent hops or wool shoddy, and, in the last resort, because it's expensive, peat or composted bark.

I'm a great believer in muck, so I went a bit mad and spread a layer about 3 in. (7.5 cm.) thick over the area to be grassed. Then I cultivated it to a depth of about 6 in. (15 cm.). Because the grass area was fairly big, and I was in a hurry (I *always* seem to be in a hurry), I did the cultivation with a big rotavator. I have one of my own for the trial ground, but, in fact, they can be hired quite cheaply, and they save a tremendous amount of work. On small areas, of course, the land can be dug by hand.

If the land is well-drained, 6 in. (15 cm.) is quite deep enough for the lawn area. On heavy soil, I would advise working in a layer of fly ash which can be bought from a power station. On really sticky stuff it's even worth putting down a 3 in. (7.5 cm.) layer of ash and covering it with the same depth of topsoil.

The next step was to mark out the lawn area. If it is to be sown, it's best to leave the area just a little wider than you want it. It can then be cut back later to leave a really good, firm edge.

For the area that is to be planted, 6 in. (15 cm.) is not deep enough. Here, it is well worth the extra effort of double digging. Certainly it's hard work, but remember that, once there are permanent plants in the borders, it will be impossible to cultivate deeply again. It *is* possible to single dig and then to dig out special holes for the plants, digging manure into the bottom, but I don't like it. Especially on heavy soils, those holes then tend to act like a sump. All the surrounding water drains into

the hole, and the plants have to suffer wet, cold feet. No one likes that.

So, I set to and double dug the borders, digging out all the buried rubbish at the same time. From one tiny border, I dug out thirty barrowloads of hardcore, no less. I left the edges of the borders nearest the lawn undug because digging would only cause sinkage round the edges of the lawn, so it was best to do this later when the grass had got a hold.

The areas to be paved consisted of hardcore, gravel, coal ash from the house fires, the odd bicycle frame and goodness knows what. Had it been good topsoil, I would have dug out those areas first and used the soil to make up the levels elsewhere.

Some of the other features, like the scree garden and the stepping stone path, I realised would have to wait. I would not have time to think about them in the first year and in any case, to tell you the truth, the budget was becoming a bit stretched by this time. In the meantime, I decided to grass over the whole area so that at least it looked tidy and would take less maintenance.

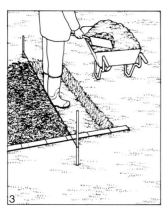

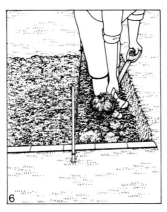

3 To double-dig, take out a trench about 2 ft. (60 cm.) wide and one spade deep

4 Put the soil into a wheelbarrow and cart it to the other end of the plot

5 Put a layer of well-rotted manure or garden compost into the bottom of the trench

6 Fork in the manure, digging down to the full depth of the fork to break up the subsoil

7 The soil from the second trench is used to fill the first and so on down the plot

FENCING AND HEDGING

The pros and cons

Most gardens need some form of boundary whether it be for privacy; to screen an ugly view; as a windbreak or simply to mark the edge of the property. A fence or a hedge of some sort is almost inevitable. Barnsdale is no exception, and I have had to build fences and plant hedging around most of the garden.

Each method of screening has its snags and its advantages. Perhaps the greatest 'plus' in favour of fencing is that it is an instant solution. You can bang up a fence round the average-sized garden in no more than a couple of days, while even the fastest hedging plants will take a few years to provide an effective screen. Fencing also has the advantage that it takes up very little growing space. In a small garden, this could be important, though on the other hand, a tall fence round a small garden does rather tend to give the impression of living in a wooden box! Still, there is nothing to stop you growing climbing plants over the fence to reduce the box effect.

The real disadvantage of fencing is that firstly, it's relatively expensive and needs maintenance and eventual replacement, and secondly, it makes an almost useless windbreak.

When wind meets a solid screen, it tends to whoosh up over the top and straight down the other side. This creates eddies and actually has the effect of increasing the wind speed only a few feet from the fence. Hedging, on the other hand, doesn't try to stop the wind dead. If filters it through its foliage, reducing the speed to a much more acceptable level, though this, of course, will depend upon the thickness of the hedge.

All hedging takes a relatively long time to make a screen, takes up a larger area of growing space, and needs regular maintenance. Don't think you can just plant a hedge and then forget about it. Like any other plant, it needs looking after if it is going to give of its best.

On the other hand, hedges make a much, much more attractive screen and you can select your plants for just the effect you want. Some plants can be used to give a foliage background to trees, shrubs and flowers, while others can give a superb flowering display themselves.

If you are looking for a really impenetrable barrier to keep out unwanted visitors, whether in human or animal form, try one of the more prickly subjects. I have a screen of *Berberis julianae* that I'm convinced would discourage a battalion of tanks!

But, perhaps the greatest advantage of all is that while fences are gradually deteriorating, hedging is continually growing bigger and better. It takes a bit of patience, but that's what gardening is all about.

Fencing

At Barnsdale, where I needed an instant screen, I used ordinary panel fencing. You can buy it at almost any garden centre, timber merchant or building supplier. But there are panels and panels. Cheap fencing is undoubtedly a false economy. I have seen some of the thinner, interwoven panels broken within a couple of weeks of going up, by footballs belted into them by budding young Kevin Keegans. If you can guarantee that they will not receive that sort of maltreatment, they are fine. Otherwise, and especially if you have children, go for the heavier overlap panels.

Though it will cost a few pounds more, it also makes sense to buy cedar, rather than softwood panels. Softwood needs annual treatment with a timber preservative – a very awkward job if you intend to grow climbers up the fence.

Posts should be of 3 in. × 3 in. (7.5 cm. × 7.5 cm.), timber and 2 ft (60 cm.) longer than the height of the fence. Never, never buy oak posts because these days, alas, the timber is kiln-dried, and it will almost certainly twist and bend out of all recognition. Unfortunately, when the posts bend, they tend to take the panels with them. It is much better to use cedar posts or, if the budget is becoming stretched, tanalised softwood. Tanalising is a process of treatment under pressure, and should guarantee the posts for the life of the fence at least.

You'll also need ballast and cement. Don't expect to get away with ramming a few bricks round the posts to hold them upright. Even low fences present quite a resistance to wind and the first strong blow will certainly move them, if not scatter them far and wide.

A few 3 in. (7.5 cm.) and 2 in. (5 cm.) oval nails completes the materials list.

When you order the fencing, by the way, don't forget to allow for the width of the posts. All those three inches added together could save you a panel, especially on a long fence.

It's quite unlikely that the space for fencing will exactly correspond with the length of the panels. You will almost certainly need one short one at the end. Some fencing manufacturers will make up a special panel to fit, but you should delay ordering this until you need it. You only need to be an inch out either way, and you're in trouble. The easiest way in any case, is to buy a complete panel and cut it to fit. It's not a difficult job.

When you come to put up the fencing, never make the mistake of setting all the posts first and fitting the panels later. This always leads to disaster. The only way to make sure of a really tight fit between panels and posts is to put up both as you go along.

The very first job is to mark out clearly your boundary. This could be much more important than you think. You may get on very well with your present neighbour, but, if he were to move away, the next one may not be so co-operative. I have known legal tussles over just two inches of land along the boundary, so it's worth being on the safe side. The deeds of the house should show them.

Mark out the boundary with a tight garden line, and dig the first hole at one end. The holes should be a little less than 2 ft (60 cm.) deep for any fence over 3 ft (1 m.) high. Below that, you can get away with 1½ ft (45 cm.) in the ground.

Place the post in the ground and measure the required height with a panel held against it. The panel should be held a couple of inches off the ground to prevent contact with the soil and subsequent rotting. I generally rest it on a house brick. There should also be about 2 in. (5 cm.) above the panel to make the job look neat once the post-caps are nailed on. If you have decided to use 'gravel-boards' under the fence, the panel should be raised the

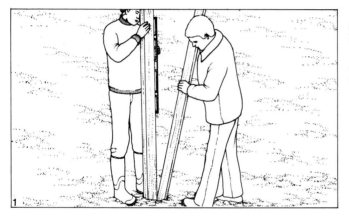

1 Set the first post in the hole and concrete it in so that it is level and at the right height

2 Measure with the panel-capping or with the panel, and dig the second hole

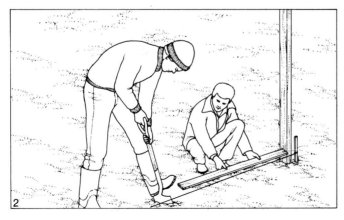

same height as the gravel board. Gravel boards are a very good idea in that they undoubtedly save the fencing panel itself from rotting. They are particularly useful if the ground slopes and the fence has to be 'stepped'. If soil lies against the boards, they may eventually rot, but they can be replaced much more cheaply than the whole panel.

With the post at the right height, it can be concreted in. Use a 6:1 mixture of $\frac{3}{4}$ in. (2 cm.) 'all-in' ballast (i.e. a mixture of sharp sand and gravel), and cement, and mix it as dry as you can, consistent with workability. Ram the concrete well down around the post, and then check with a spirit-level that it is perfectly upright both ways.

Now, using the panel as a marker, measure out and dig the second hole as before. Once this hole is dug to about the right depth, the first panel can be nailed to the first post. Use 3 in. (7.5 cm.) oval nails, nailing both sides of the panel. The other end of the panel will have to be supported again to the right height, while this job is being done.

3 Nail the panel to the first post and check that it is level

4 Measure the height of the second post with a small block of wood

The second post can now be put in the hole and checked for height. I cut a piece of wood the same length as the distance between the top of the panel and the top of the post. Then all you have to do is to place it on the top of the panel and adjust the post to the required depth. When it's right, nail the second panel to the post and concrete it in as before. Check again with the spirit level that both posts are upright both ways.

While the concrete is setting, the panels must be supported to prevent them moving. I do this by propping them with spare posts or lengths of timber.

Now continue down the line in the same way. When the end is reached, it is unlikely that the last panel will fit. If it does – nip out to the betting shop quickly – it's obviously your lucky day!

Place the last post in position and measure accurately the space between the two posts. The panel can now be cut to fit.

Start by levering off the framework at one end. This is then re-nailed onto the panel in the correct position. Then the excess is cut off and the panel should fit exactly between the two posts.

5 Nail the panel to the second post, and concrete it in, checking that it is upright

6 As each panel is fixed, support it with a spare post or a length of timber

Gravel boards, if you are using them, are fitted last. Cut a few blocks of wood the same length as the width of the gravel board and nail them to the posts underneath the panels. The gravel boards are then cut to length and, in turn, nailed to the blocks.

Stepped fencing

Panel fencing can't be sloped, so if the ground slopes, it will have to be stepped. Start from the highest end and set the first post and panel as before. The second post is now fitted to the first panel. When the second panel is nailed to the other side of the second post, set it so that it too is 2 in. (5 cm.) off the ground. This will put it some way below the level of the first panel. Continue down the slope in this way but, for the neatest job, try to make the 'step' exactly the same in every case. Gravel boards should be fitted when panels are stepped, burying one end in the soil with the other just a little above it. When all the posts and panels are up and the concrete has set, remove the supporting posts and nail the caps to the posts using 2 in. (5 cm.) oval nails.

7 To fix gravel boards, first nail a block of wood underneath the panel

8 Nail on the board, so that the nails go into the block and into the post

One word of warning: try not to buy creosoted panels, because their fumes will kill plants on or near the fence. If that is all that's available, wait several weeks before planting.

Hedging

Hedges can be neatly divided into two categories – the formal and the informal. Formal hedges are clipped or pruned from once to four or five times a year depending on their rate of growth. This maintains a neat, wall-like appearance and takes up less room than an informal hedge. These consist of flowering shrubs which are more or less left to grow to their natural shape. Obviously much more growing space is required for an informal hedge.

At Barnsdale, I have planted both types. A formal conifer hedge serves to hide the unsightly workshop area on one side of the garden, while a prickly informal barrier on the road side prevents, or at least discourages, the local population of cats, dogs, sheep, cows and people who tend to show an interest in my prized collection of plants.

I chose a conifer for the formal hedge because it is relatively fast-growing, evergreen and dense enough to act as an effective windbreak. I thought long and hard about the variety. *Cupresso ×
cyparis leylandii* is undoubtedly the fastest-growing and makes a good, hardy hedge, but in the end, I settled for *Thuja plicata
'Atrovirens'*. Though slightly slower-growing, it has a bright glossy sheen to its foliage that I find very attractive. Far from distracting from the shrubs planted in front if it, it seems to light them up with a bright green glow.

There are plenty of other hedging plants to choose from and I have listed here some of my favourites that might suit your garden better.

Conifers

Chamaecyparis lawsoniana 'Allumii', bluish-grey and green foliage make this an attractive hedge. It's a bit expensive and not as fast as many of the green foliage conifers. In ten years it will, under good conditions, reach about 8 ft (2.5 m.). Plant 3–4 ft (90–120 cm.) apart.

Cupressocyparis leylandii is the fastest-growing of the conifers and should grow about 2–3 ft (60–90 cm.) a year once it has become established. The foliage is matt green and perhaps a little dull, though it makes a good neutral background for other plants. There are several different 'clones', or mother plants of *leylandii*, so it's worth shopping around for one with a close, bushy habit. In ten years, it should reach about 12–15 ft (3.5–4.5 m.). Plant 3 ft (90 cm.) apart.

Cupressocyparis leylandii 'Castlewellan' is the golden form of *leylandii*. It grows just a little slower and is fine where you need a

Thuja plicata 'Atrovirens'

really bright hedge. For me, it's just a bit too garish, especially if it is to be used as a backing to other plants.

Thuja plicata 'Atrovirens' is the one I used at Barnsdale and which I like the best. It should be planted 3 ft (90 cm.) apart.

Taxus baccata, the Yew, is a traditional hedging plant used widely in the gardens of stately homes. It can be clipped closely to make a really superb formal hedge. It is slower-growing than the other conifers I have mentioned, but well worth the wait if you have the patience. The matt green foliage makes a perfect

25

background to other planting. It will reach about 6 ft (1.8 m.) in ten years if grown well. Plant 2 ft (60 cm.) apart.

Other formal hedges

Fagus sylvatica, the Common Beech, makes an excellent hedge which will be attractive throughout the year. Though not ever-green, it retains its brown leaves through the winter until they are pushed off by the young growth. The purple form is perhaps even more attractive. It's a bit slow-growing, but again, worth patience. Plant 1½ ft (45 cm.) apart. *Carpinus betulus*, the Horn-beam is very much like beech, but easier to establish on heavy soils, and a little faster.

Crataegus oxyacantha, Quickthorn, makes a fast, thorny hedge, but is not evergreen. It is used widely in the country as a field hedge where it makes a good animal barrier. It can be used in rural gardens, but is not the most attractive hedge in the world. Plant 1 ft (30 cm.) apart.

Ligustrum ovalifolium is the Latin name for privet which makes a fine, formal hedge and is often evergreen, especially in the south. It has one big disadvantage. Being very hungry indeed, it takes up a lot of growing space and should therefore really only be used in large gardens. Plant 1 ft (30 cm.) apart.

Prunus laurocerasus 'Rotundifolia', the glossy green leaved Laurel, makes a very attractive formal, or semi-formal hedge. It must be pruned with secateurs rather than shears, to avoid unsightly cut leaves. Plant 2 ft (60 cm.) apart.

Informal hedges

Berberis darwinii is a good prickly one if you need an impenetrable barrier. The three-pointed, glossy green leaves are evergreen, and it produces an abundance of deep yellow flowers in April/May. These are followed by dark purple berries. Plant 2 ft (60 cm.) apart.

Mixed pyracantha varieties

Berberis julianae is not often recommended as a hedging plant but I have found it excellent. The spines on this variety are really vicious, so be careful where you plant it. It has a very dense habit and long, glossy evergreen leaves which are tinged red when young and turn a deeper red in autumn. The flowers are deep yellow and slightly scented. Plant 2 ft (60 cm.) apart.

Berberis stenophylla – this one needs a bit more room, because the branches arch over in a most attractive way. In April/May, it bears masses of deep yellow flowers.

Escallonia is the flowering hedge for you if you live near the seaside. There are many types ranging in colour from white, through pink to red, and all of them are evergreen. Plant 2½ ft (75 cm.) apart.

Osmarea burkwoodii is a compact-growing evergreen with lus-trous green leaves and the considerable bonus of small, white

Above: *Pyracantha watereri*

Above right: *Berberis darwinii*

flowers in April/May, that are really heavily scented. Plant 2 ft (60 cm.) apart.

Rhododendron ponticum or the common rhododendron, is a familiar hedging shrub in areas where the soil is acid. They will not do well on chalky soil. The large evergreen leaves make it an attractive sight and an excellent screen all the year. The flowers are pinky-mauve and very spectacular. This is a hedging shrub for large gardens only, since it tends to grow big and to sprawl. Plant 3 ft (90 cm.) apart.

Pyracantha rogersiana, the Firethorn, is usually grown as a wall shrub, but makes an excellent hedging plant too. The leaves are evergreen and the white flowers are followed by masses of bright red berries. It will grow and thrive almost anywhere. Plant 2 ft (60 cm.) apart.

Viburnum tinus, this well-known Laurustinus makes an excellent, dense, evergreen hedge. It bears clusters of pink buds

27

in late winter and early spring, which open to white and pink flowers followed by deep blue berries. The variety Eve Price is one of the best. Plant 2 ft (60 cm.) apart.

Hedge planting

The whole essence of growing a hedge, is to do it quickly. The sooner the plants are performing their function of screening or windbreaking, the better, therefore it's worth taking a little extra trouble to give them the best conditions possible.

The soil at Barnsdale is very light, so it was important to enrich it with a generous helping of organic matter. In fact, the same sort of preparation would have served if the soil was on the heavy side, to open it up and give the roots a good, easy way downwards.

A good root system is all important with hedging plants, especially if they are to be allowed to grow tall. I have seen very large conifers simply blown out of the soil because the anchorage was insufficient.

I started off by marking out and digging a trench $1\frac{1}{2}$ ft (45 cm.) wide and one spade deep. The soil at the bottom of the trench was broken up to the depth of the fork, so the roots would have a really easy time getting through the otherwise hard layer just below the topsoil.

Then I put in a layer about 2 in. (5 cm.) deep, of well-rotted farmyard manure. If you can't get hold of it, use compost, mushroom manure or one of the alternatives. This layer I forked into the bottom of the trench. When doing this, it's important not to bring too much subsoil up to the surface, though in my opinion, a little does no harm.

On top of that layer, I then put another 3 in. (7.5 cm.) of muck. On the soil I had dug out of the trench, I sprinkled a general fertiliser. I like blood, fish and bone for this job because, being organic, it tends to last a bit longer in the soil. Use about a

1 Dig out a trench about $1\frac{1}{2}$ ft (45 cm.) wide and one spade deep, down the run of the hedge

2 Fork over the bottom to the depth of the fork and put in a layer of manure or compost

3 If roots of potted plants spiral round the pot, gently tease them out

4 Cut out a slit with the spade and put in the plant so that the roots hang downwards

5 Hold the plant upright and consolidate the soil round the roots with your boot

handful for every 1 yd (90 cm.) run. The trench was then refilled.

To make a really good job of it, I then forked yet another layer of manure into the top levels of the soil. If those plants weren't grateful to me, they jolly well should have been.

Now the trench must be allowed to settle. When it is refilled, with the extra manure and with breaking it up, it will be mounded up quite a lot, so there will be plenty of room for sinkage. I left mine for three weeks before planting.

If the plants are in containers, they can be planted at any time of the year. Generally, conifers and the more exotic shrubs that are used for hedging can be bought in small pots. However, the cheaper subjects like quickthorn or privet are generally sold bare-rooted. These must be planted in the dormant season. The best time for deciduous subjects is when the leaves have fallen and this means any time between November and March. However, it's much better to plant before Christmas if possible. There is a little warmth left in the soil up to then, so the roots should make some growth before winter sets in. Evergreens are best set during September/October or again in April or early May.

The plants I used at Barnsdale, were all in small pots. There is very little point, incidentally, in buying large plants in big containers for hedging. The younger ones will get away much faster and will soon catch them up. They will also grow uniformly and produce a much better hedge in the long run.

There is one important point to watch when buying plants in pots. If they have been potted a little overlong, the roots reach the bottom and then tend to run round the bottom of the pot. Some plants, particularly conifers, seem to continue this trend even when they are planted out. For some reason, they get into the habit of growing in a circular fashion and find it difficult to 'kick'. So, when the plant is knocked out of the pot, have a look at the root system. If they are running around the bottom, they must be gently teased out. If this is not done, there is an increased

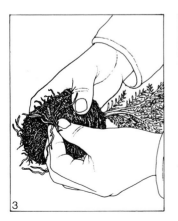
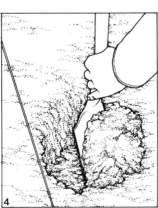

chance that the plants will blow over when they get bigger. Of course, a certain amount of root damage does occur. But this is infinitely preferable to the disaster of a whole hedge leaning over in high winds.

Planting in the prepared trench is an easy matter. Start by running a line down the centre of the trench as a guide. Then push the space into the soft soil, more or less at right-angles to your body. A slight twist will make a hole large enough to take the roots.

Potted plants can simply be placed in the hole, but bare-rooted ones should be put in with a quick flick of the wrist to ensure that the roots hang downwards and are not bunched up. Then, making sure the plants are at the level they grew in the nursery, simply remove the spade and firm the roots in with your heel.

If, after planting, the soil is dry, be prepared to water by hand. In hot weather, or in high winds, the foliage of evergreens, particularly conifers will lose water very rapidly. In this case, it is wise to spray water over the tops of the plants at regular intervals. If this is impossible, apply a transplanting spray. This covers the leaves with a thin film of plastic and prevents excessive water-loss.

Windbreaks

If you have planted a hedge to serve as a windbreak, as I did at Barnsdale, there is one obvious problem. The hedging plants are there to protect the remainder of the plants in the garden from the damaging effects of high winds. But what protects the windbreak? I planted conifers which are, because of their large leaf area, particularly prone to rapid drying-out of the foliage, resulting in ugly leaf scorch, and generally a bare length of stem at the bottom.

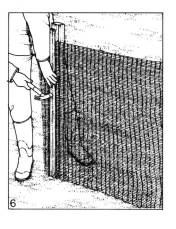

The only real answer is to erect a temporary windscreen. I used a special plastic netting but a length of hessian will do as well. Obviously, the supporting posts must be firmly set in the ground, and it may be necessary to put guy-ropes on the windward side to prevent the screen blowing over. It should only be necessary to leave the windscreen in position until the plants have rooted and are capable of transporting water quickly to the foliage to replace excessive transpiration. Windbreaks of plastic or hessian are not, in my opinion, a pretty sight, but they are essential if you are going to get your hedge off to a good start.

6 A temporary windscreen of plastic or hessian will help avoid wind damage

Aftercare

Though you will have to steel yourself to do it, it is best to cut some hedging plants right back hard after planting. Quickthorn and privet will benefit greatly from this sort of treatment, forming a much more bushy hedge. Others can be trimmed back during the following and subsequent seasons, also to make them bushy, while some should not be pruned at all for the first few years.

Conifers should be left alone until they have reached their required height. Early cutting back results in forking of the leading shoot and this makes for an untidy and gappy hedge. When it is as high as is needed, the top and the sides can be trimmed annually and the best month to do this is August. As with all hedges, the best way to trim the sides is to cut back to form a wide base narrowing at the top. This allows light to reach the foliage all the way down, and generally avoids dying back and resulting bareness at the bottom.

Hornbeam and beech hedges are also best left alone for the first couple of years at least. After that, they too can be trimmed back annually in the same way, cutting back the sides but letting the leading shoot grow on until it reaches the required height.

Laurel and all the informal hedges can be trimmed lightly during the spring after planting. This job is best done with secateurs rather than shears. Trim the flowering hedges immediately after flowering, cutting out the older shoots.

For some reason I have never understood, hedges tend to get left out when the nose-bag is going around the garden. They need feeding just as much as any other plant. More perhaps, because we are expecting some pretty rapid growth, at least in the early stages. Generally, it will only be necessary to feed them once a year. I give mine a dressing of blood, fish and bone at the end of February, applying it at about 4 oz per sq.yd (120 gm per sq.m.). At the same time, it's a good idea to thoroughly clean the weeds away from the bottom of the hedge, and spread a couple of inches of manure or compost.

Weeding is important especially around young hedging plants. Every weed will compete with the plants for food and water and will reduce the speed of growth. Either hoe them out or spray carefully round the base of the plants with paraquat (ICI Weedol) if the weeds are annuals, or glyphosate (Murphy Tumbleweed), in the case of perennials. After the plants have been established a couple of years, I prefer to use Casaron G for weed control. This comes in granular form, so there is no fear of spray-drift onto the plants, and the effect lasts longer.

PAVING AND WALLING

Gardens should not always be hard work. Of course, there's never a moment when there's nothing to do, and I know that I'm always fidgeting about wanting to get on with some job or other. But, what better, at the end of a long summer day in the garden, than to relax and just enjoy it. When the weather's good, I spend as much time in the fresh air as I possibly can. I'm lucky to have a real sun-trap corner, sheltered on three sides by walls, where I can sit and make the most of the summer sun. That area simply had to be paved, so that I could set out the table and chairs permanently, without having to shift them about every time I wanted to mow the lawn.

Paving is not cheap, of course, and there are certainly easier jobs in the garden. So, I felt it was essential to get it right first time. There are no short cuts and trying to save on materials or labour is, in my opinion, a false economy.

Do the job properly, and you'll have an attractive feature that will last you a lifetime.

Choice of paving

I suppose that the traditionalists would insist that a proper cottage-garden must be covered with crazy-paving. Frankly, I think it's *awful*. Around a little thatched cottage in the country, with roses round the door and all that, it looks at home. Around a new house, built with modern materials it's about as fitting as Attila the Hun at the Mother's Union!

My cottage at Barnsdale is, I suppose, in between the two, but I certainly felt that rectangular slabs would fit in best. But one must beware of going too far in the opposite direction. Square concrete slabs laid in regular lines look like the council car-park and are much too formal. I settled for rectangular paving in different sizes, laid in a random pattern.

There are several different finishes and materials to choose from and the final choice should depend upon the materials marrying with the house itself. Of course, on personal preference, I would very much like to have settled for old York stone paving, but when I found out the price, I instantly changed my mind. Instead, I chose an imitation York slab, with a 'riven' finish. It looks very much like the real thing.

There are two other important factors to bear in mind. Firstly, if you anticipate having to cut several slabs, it is best to buy something that will cut with a hammer and brick-bolster. If the wall of your house is dead straight, and there are no inspection covers to negotiate, concrete slabs are fine. But cutting concrete really needs a stone saw which is quite expensive to hire. If your

Right: a collection of plants brighten up a paved area and soften the hard lines

Plants will often sow themselves in the cracks between paving. They may need to be kept in check

supplier can't tell you whether the slabs will cut by hand, try one. He's bound to have the odd broken bit you can use. Natural stone slabs will generally cut quite easily, and so will those made from reconstituted natural stone.

If you are laying paving in a shaded or damp spot, it is likely to become covered in algae growth. This makes it very slippery and quite dangerous. In this case, choose a slab with a non-slip finish.

The best way to order slabs is to measure up the area and ask the merchant to supply the required amount in square yards or preferably metres, since they are all made in metric sizes these days. Allow a few extra for breakages, especially if you will need to cut some. You're bound to have the odd mishap.

If you decide to use random rectangular paving, you'll need to order the different sizes you need. The easiest way is to ask for equal amounts in square yards, *not* equal numbers, or you'll finish up with far too many big slabs.

It will also be necessary to order ballast for the base and soft sand for bedding the slabs. Depending on how firm the base is, you'll generally get away with 3 in. (7.5 cm.) of concrete, so for every 12 sq.yds of base area, you'll need 1 cubic yd of 'all-in' ballast. Each cubic yard will need about eight bags of Portland cement. These figures are, of course, only approximate but will not leave you far out.

Preparation

Unless the soil on which paving is to be laid has been consolidated over a number of years, an adequate concrete base must be laid.

This is especially so with new houses, when the paving is to be laid close to the wall. These days, footings are dug out much wider than necessary, because they depend upon the size of the digger bucket. They are later refilled with soil after the house has been built. However much it may be consolidated, that soil will *always* sink. If the paving is laid on sand, it will sink too, leaving your prized patio uneven and dangerous. The only way to be sure is to lay the slabs on concrete.

At Barnsdale, the ground I was going to pave was solid hardcore. That would have been fine if it had been at the right level. As it was, I had to dig out load after load of old bricks and stones before I reached the required depth. It really is important to put the paving at least two courses of bricks below the damp-proof course of the house. If you don't, water from the paving may seep through the bricks and up the walls, playing havoc with the wallpaper inside! So, dig out, you must. The damp-proof course can be easily recognised on new houses, by a wider bed of mortar between bricks.

At Barnsdale, as on many older houses, it consists of a row of blue engineering bricks.

So, the first job is to dig out roughly to the correct levels. This will depend upon the thickness of your paving slabs. If you use 2 in. (5 cm.) slabs, you must allow for them, plus 1 in. (2.5 cm.)

1 Start by digging out the base to roughly the correct levels

2 Mark a line on the pegs at the level the concrete will finish

3 Set the pegs at the right level, using a straight-edge and spirit-level

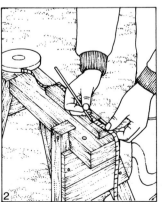

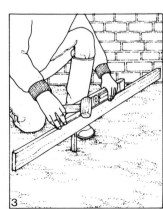

of mortar for bedding them, and at least 3 in. (7.5 cm.) of concrete. That makes 6 in. (15 cm.) in all below the course of bricks, two below the damp-proof course. I in fact, wanted to leave a border between the paving and the house, but I still dug down to those levels to avoid the border sloping backwards. It wouldn't do to pile the soil up above the damp-proof course, either.

Now the whole area must be pegged out accurately. Use some good, stout pegs, at least 1 ft (30 cm.) long, because maintaining the correct levels is all important. Before banging them in, mark a line on them to show where the concrete level should come. This will be $2\frac{1}{2}$ in. (6.5 cm.) from the top of the peg if you are using $1\frac{1}{2}$ in. (4 cm.) paving, and 3 in. (7.5 cm.) for 2 in. (5 cm.) slabs.

Bang in the first peg near the wall and level it with a spirit level, so that the top of the peg comes parallel with the row of bricks two below the damp-proof course. Now put in a row of pegs fairly near to the wall and in line with the first peg, which will also act as the level indicator.

The next row of pegs should line up with the first and should be about 4 ft (120 cm.) away. These must be set a little lower than the first row, in order to ensure that the paving slopes away from the house a little. The slope need be only very slight – just enough to ensure that rainwater doesn't run backwards towards the house. The way to do it, is to bang the peg in roughly to the right level, and then place a block of wood $\frac{1}{2}$ in. (13 mm.) thick on top. Now level the peg in with the corresponding one in the first row. Remove the block, and the peg is at the right level. The second row can be levelled in from this peg. When it comes to the third and subsequent rows, the same technique will ensure that the slope is even throughout.

When all the pegs are in and levelled, check that there are not any high spots of soil. If there are, scrape them off. Low patches should not be refilled with soil, as this may also sink.

4 Cover the base area with concrete a little higher than the required finish level

5 Consolidate so that the final level is no higher than the mark on the pegs

6 Set the outside circle of bricks using a line tied to the centre peg

Mix the concrete for the base in a ratio of six parts by volume of ballast to one of cement. The base I was working on was quite hard, so I mixed the concrete dry. Later, the moisture from the soil below and the rain above was enough to harden it. However, on soft soil, I would prefer to use a wet mix, to form a complete concrete raft, to avoid sinking. You can't be too careful.

The concrete is levelled in to the mark on the pegs and firmed down well. Then the base is ready for the paving. Just one word of warning. When levelling, make sure that the concrete is, if anything, below the line on the pegs. It is better to be too low than too high, or the slabs will not go down level. Also, in the interest of safety, it is as well to rope off the area you are working on, just to make quite sure that nobody walks across it. Those pegs will be sticking up a couple of inches and can be quite dangerous.

Paving

The paved area in my garden was edged with bricks in order to link with the main feature – the scree garden. The bricks were laid flat, in a semi-circle on the outside edge of the paving, and the slabs were cut into the curve. It was therefore essential to choose a paving that would cut easily. I must say that this is not the easiest job, and takes a bit of practice. If you haven't done it before, it is probably an economy to hire a stone saw. Otherwise, breakages can be high and so can tempers!

It's important to get the right bricks, too. I was lucky; there were several blue engineering bricks in the garden, ideal for the job and very attractive. If you have to buy them, you must make sure that you select bricks that will not deteriorate quickly when laid flat. Most bricks used for walling are made to be used upright, so that they shed rainwater. If water lies on ordinary fletton bricks, or on the sand-faced flettons used generally for house-building these days, they will quickly flake. In the winter, the water penetrates the porous brick and, when it freezes, the surface will rapidly crumble. Engineering bricks are much harder so water will not penetrate. Unfortunately, they are also much more expensive, but you may be able to find some secondhand ones in the local demolition contractor's yard.

When marking out the area to be paved, I marked the circle simply by banging in a peg, attaching a piece of cord and scratching a mark in the soil with another peg tied to the other end. I retained that central peg in position, so all I had to do was to re-tie the string to be able to make an accurate semi-circle with the bricks. The string is used, not only to mark the outside edge of the circle, but also to ensure that each brick faces into the centre of the circle.

The bricks are bedded into a mortar made with three parts of

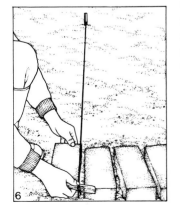

6

37

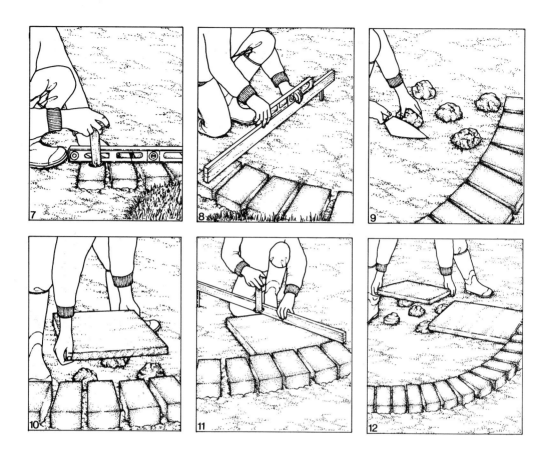

soft, builders' sand to one part of cement, mixed fairly dry. The same mixture is used for bedding the slabs.

Using the level pegs to ensure that the bricks are at the correct height, and the string to align them, it is a simple matter to form the brick semi-circle.

When laying the slabs, the first one is all-important, since it sets the level and line for the remainder.

It's worth spending a lot of time and trouble to ensure that this one is dead right. If it is, the others will follow easily. If the slabs are to be laid next to the house wall, start near the wall. They are set on five heaps of mortar, one in each corner of the slab and one in the middle. Make the heaps about 3 in. (7.5 cm.) or more high, to give plenty of room to tap the slab down level.

Set the slab about 1 in. (2.5 cm.) away from the wall and then set a line so that it runs exactly along the edge. Run the line right to the other end of the run of paving, about 1 in. (2.5 cm.) away from the house wall and then move the slab so that it's exactly in line with it. A deviation of only a fraction of an inch will put the

7 Set the bricks on a bed of mortar and level them in with a spirit-level

8 Check that they are perfectly level using a straight-edge onto the top of the level-pegs

9 The first slab is set on five points of mortar mixed to a fairly dry consistency

10 Gently place the slab on top of the heaps of mortar

11 Using the straight-edge, gently tap the slab down to the correct level

12 Subsequent slabs are laid in the same way, butting them up together

13 To cut slabs, first lay one in position and mark the line of the cut

14 Cut a nick in the edge of the slab and mark a line on the other side

15 Resting the slab against your leg, gently tap both sides until it falls into two pieces

16 The cut slab can now be set into position and tapped down level

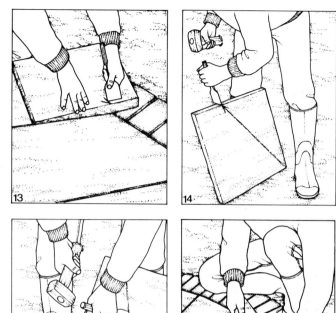

paving inches out at the other end of the run. When it is exactly lined up, it can be tapped down level.

To do this, put a long straight-edge on the slab, and onto the top of the nearest peg. Tap the slab down with the handle of a club-hammer, until the straight-edge lies flat on it. Then check the other direction with the straight-edge on another peg. Take time and trouble to ensure that this slab is perfectly level and in line. It'll save hours of frustration later.

It's worth checking again, just to make sure that the process of levelling has not put the slab out of line with the wall, and then the rest of the paving can be laid. While some people prefer to point in between slabs, I like to simply butt them up together. Indeed, it's a good idea to leave a gap of about $\frac{1}{4}$ in. (6 mm.), to allow plants to grow there. There are several alpine species that will do well in even a tiny amount of soil and these do much to soften the hard lines of the paving.

When laying the main bulk of the slabs, a little forethought is required to avoid long 'tramlines'. Think a couple of slabs ahead and if a line seems to be getting too long, break it by using a slab of a different size across the line.

Here and there, it is also a good idea to leave a small space in the paving for planting rather larger alpines or even dwarf conifers. I left squares 6 in. × 6 in. (15 cm. × 15 cm.), filled them with compost and planted them with thymes, alpine hypericum and campanulas. If you do this, it makes sense to plant the larger subjects in a spot that will not otherwise be used.

Inspection covers

If you are making your paved area near the house, you'll be very lucky indeed if you don't encounter at least one inspection cover. These are the cast iron lids used to cover the manholes, necessary for inspecting the drainage system from the house. If you get a blockage in the drains, it may be essential to get at that manhole, so they must on no account be covered.

For some reason unknown to Man the builders rarely, if ever, put them in either square with the house, or at the correct level, so they invariably have to be moved. Fear not – it's not a difficult job at all.

I had two, right outside the back door, and they were all over the place, neither level nor square. Now, they are hardly noticeable.

I like to leave the adjustment of the covers until I have paved nearly up to them. That way, you can be sure of getting them dead level with the paving, and you may be able to save yourself a bit of slab-cutting by moving the cover a little. Certainly, you'll be able to square up the cover with the paving.

When the paving has reached as near to the cover as possible, the first job is to remove the top, and knock out the frame. This is the metal rectangle that the cover fits onto. It is generally made of cast iron, so a little care is needed, since they crack easily. It should come out fairly easily with a few well-judged taps with a hammer and cold chisel.

If the frame needs raising a fair way, it can be done by setting another course of bricks. If it needs to come up less than this, either cut off the 'frog' – the indented part of the brick – or use a few old roofing tiles. At the same time, the cover can be adjusted slightly to make it square with the paving. It doesn't matter if it looks a bit messy inside, since the cover will prevent it being seen.

If you want to make a really good job, it is possible to buy a 'Broads' cover. This is no more than a metal frame which can be filled with concrete coloured with a cement additive to match the paving. Done well, the cover then becomes virtually unnoticeable. When all the paving is down, all that remains is to point in along the wall. Make sure also, that you prevent anybody treading on the slabs for at least a couple of days.

Walls

The ornamental walls at Barnsdale are made with a reconstituted natural stone, to match the paving. If you can't find a stone that is exactly the same, it is better, in my opinion, to go for something completely different, like brick, rather than something that almost matches, but not quite. That always looks like a near miss.

Artificial stone comes either 'dressed' or plain. I very much prefer dressed or 'rock-faced' stone, but frankly, I like to do it myself. I have yet to find a dressed stone that is done well, and it does make all the difference.

Plants tumbling over retaining walls turn them into an attractive feature

All that is involved is chipping off the front edges of the stone, to make the face stand out in relief, and then squaring up the ends. Mark a line about $\frac{1}{2}$ in. (13 mm.) from the front face of the stone and chip off the edge with a brick bolster. Then do the same thing on each end, making sure that the line is exactly at right-angles to the first line.

Then repeat the process on the other side. Check the front face to ensure that the ends are square, and the job's done. Once you get into it, you'll find that the work proceeds quite quickly.

The foundations for the wall are again made with a 6 : 1 mix of ballast and cement, but should be somewhat deeper than for paving. The depth will depend to some extent on the height of the wall, but generally 6 in. (15 cm.) is plenty for a dwarf wall.

If your wall is to be next to the paved area as mine was, you will already have determined the levels. Finish the concrete a fraction below the paving, so that it doesn't show. If not, you will have to peg it in the same way as for the paving base, with the finish level of the concrete a little below ground level.

The mortar for bedding the walling is again made with a 3 : 1 mix of soft sand and cement. Mix it quite dry for walling, since wet cement will stick to the rough faces of the stone and look ugly. For brickwork, the mortar can be wetter. Start by setting the two stones at the end of the run. Bed them on about $\frac{3}{4}$ in. (2 cm.) of mortar, and tap them down to $\frac{1}{2}$ in. (13 mm.).

Now stretch a tight line along the front edge of the stone. It's well worth buying a special, nylon bricklayer's line for this job, you'll never get a good indication of level with a bit of hairy string. For this first course, I wrap the ends of the line around one of the stones to hold it firm, and rest another on top of the stone I have laid, to hold the line in place.

With the line in place you'll be able to see whether or not the stones are straight and level. If not, gently tap them into place. Now, using the line as a guide set the remainder of the row. From time to time, put the spirit level across the stones to ensure that they are level that way too. This should ensure that the wall goes up straight.

If the wall is intended to retain soil, as mine was, it is really important to allow for 'weep-holes' in the first course. These are simply spaces left to allow water to drain out. If it is allowed to build up behind the wall, it can exert a lot of pressure and could even knock the wall down.

I got hold of a few drainage tiles from my local agricultural merchant, and set those in the holes. They're not essential, but just finish the job off nicely.

When the first course is completed, point in the spaces between the stones with mortar. There is no need to worry too much about the finish at this stage. It's best to do that at the end of the day when the mortar is getting hard.

The improved drainage provided by walling makes an ideal environment for many alpine and rock-plants

1 To 'face' walling stones, first mark a line $\frac{1}{2}$ in. (13 mm.) from the face edge

2 Mark the line right round the stone, and then chip away the top edge

3 Do the same thing on the ends and then make sure the front face is exactly square

4 Make the concrete foundation slightly lower than the level of the paving slabs

5 Mix up the mortar accurately using a bucket to ensure that each mix is the same colour

6 Set the first stone at the end of the run, tapping it down to form a $\frac{1}{2}$ in. (13 mm.) mortar joint

The second course is set in exactly the same way, but the stones on this course must be 'bonded' with the first. This is simply a matter of starting the row with half a stone, so that the centres of the stones of the second course come over the joints between those on the first.

Some manufacturers supply 'jumpers' to go with their walling. These are simply larger stones made exactly the width of two normal stones plus the depth of the mortar joint. Incorporated into a wall, they make a very pleasing, random effect. They can't be put in until the rest of the course is laid, because they would get in the way of the line, so the best way is to lay the course normally, and then remove one stone and replace it with a jumper. This is then levelled in with the next course.

When building with brick, it's easy to check that the wall is going up straight – all you need do is to put the spirit-level against the side. But stone walls are not so straightforward. They have a rough, uneven face, so it is impossible to level them in this way. Firstly, check frequently with the spirit-level laid

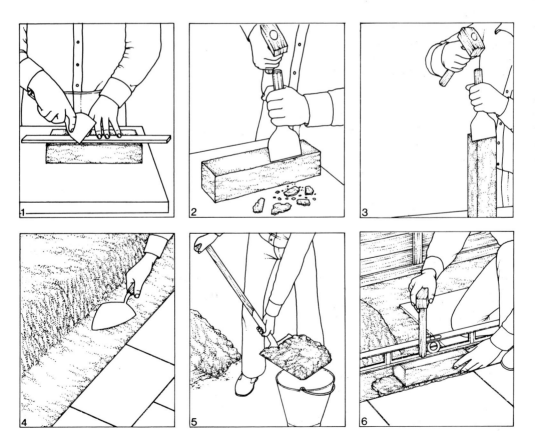

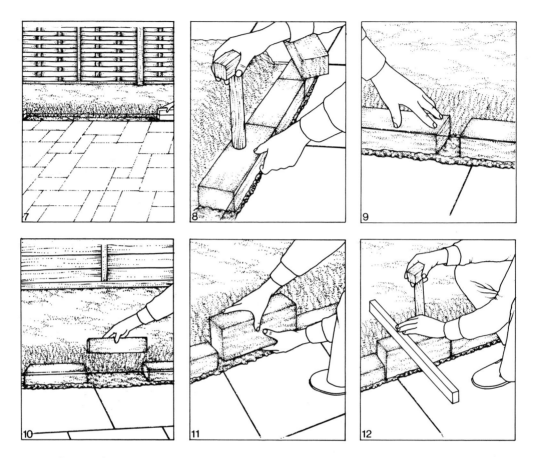

across the run of the walling, for level that way. Other than that, all you can do is to check it by eye. What I do, is to bang a stake in at one end of the wall, and make sure with the spirit-level that it is dead straight. Then it can be used as a guide for straightness when you sight along the wall.

When you have reached the required height, the top must be finished off with a coping stone. This is generally a flat slab, thinner but wider than the walling. It is set so that it overhangs the front of the wall by about 1 in. (2.5 cm.). Before setting, the coping must be 'faced' in the same way as the walling. At the same time, all the copings must be trimmed so that they are the same width. This may mean chipping a little off both sides.

From time to time, you should check to see how hard the first lot of mortar has become, though I have found that it is normally not too hard to rake out by the end of a normal working day. Don't let it get too solid though, and whatever you do, don't forget to clean up all the joints at the end of the day. If you do, it becomes a hammer and chisel job.

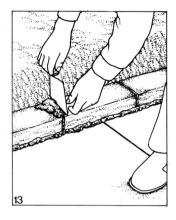

7 Set the stone at the other end and then stretch a tight line between

8 Using the line as a guide, the remaining stones in the run can now be laid

9 If the wall is to retain soil, make sure you leave some 'weepholes' in the first course

10 If you are using 'jumpers' one of the stones in the run should be removed

11 The larger 'jumper' can now be placed in position and tapped down level

12 Check for level across the length of the run to ensure that the wall is going up straight

13 After the first course has been laid, point in between the joints with mortar

14 Coping stones must be set on the top of the wall when it has reached the required height

15 Finally, rake out the mortar from the joints, cutting back about ½ in. (13 mm.)

Raking out the joints is a straightforward task, if a little tedious, but it makes all the difference to the final look of the job. It's just a case of scraping out the excess mortar from between the joints. I use a piece of wood, and I rake back to something like ½ in. (13 mm.).

If you have made your mortar a bit too wet at any time and it has fallen on the face of the walling, it too must be removed at this stage. It will come off easily with a wire brush if you catch it before it really hardens.

Then go over the whole face of the wall with a soft brush to remove any loose crumbs of mortar. Now you can sit back and indulge yourself in half-an-hour's 'admiring time'. You'll deserve it.

Steps

Garden steps are obviously necessary for access between two levels. They can also be made very attractive and used as a feature to add interest to the scheme. In my view, unless they are hidden from sight, they should never be solely utilitarian, but should always look good too.

In my garden it was necessary to provide two sets of steps, one to change the level of the paving, and the other to give access to the slightly higher lawn area. Both were leading from the paved area, so I used the same materials. For the 'risers', I actually used the same engineering bricks I had used in the paving edging, but walling stone could be used to equal effect.

When designing steps, never skimp on the space. Though it may seem a contradiction in terms, narrow steps make the garden look narrower while wide ones give the illusion of more space. The same goes for paths too.

The height of the risers should never be so much that the steps have to be climbed with effort, nor so low, that they are not readily seen or else people will be in danger of tripping.

The ideal height is about 6 in. (15 cm.), and as it happens, this works out in a very convenient way. Starting from the bottom, you allow ½ in. (13 mm.) for the mortar to bed the riser, 3 in. (7.5 cm.) for the thickness of the brick or stone, another ½ in. (13 mm.) for the mortar to bed the paving, and 1½ in. (4 cm.) for the slab. This works out to exactly 6 in. (15 cm.). If you are using 2 in. (5 cm.) thick slabs, the extra height is quite acceptable.

However, nothing is ever as simple as it looks. The height of the steps will be finally determined by the distance between the two levels. So, you may need to make a slight adjustment.

Start off by working out the difference in height between the two levels. You can do this quite easily by getting someone to hold a straight edge on the top level, making sure that it is level by putting the spirit-level on top. Now all you have to do is to measure between the bottom of the straight edge and the lower level, to find out the difference in height. Then, bearing in mind that the steps must be as near 6 in. (15 cm.) high as possible, you can work out how many you need.

Try always to make the height of each step a little less than 6 in. (15 cm.) rather than a bit more. The only way of increasing the height is to make the mortar joint thicker, and this looks ugly. If they are a little lower, the bed for the riser can be lowered by lowering the foundation a little.

Having decided on the number and the height of the steps, the first job is to dig out roughly the profile of the required slope. There is no need to be accurate.

Then put in the foundation for the first riser in exactly the way described earlier for walling. If the risers are to be say ¼ in. (6 mm.) less than the 6 in. (15 cm.) suggested, finish the top of the foundation ¼ in. (6 mm.) below the level of the adjoining paving. The first riser can then be set.

Then fill in behind the riser with concrete up to the top of the bricks and set your paving slabs on top. When this is done, the foundation for the next riser can be put in and the process repeated.

Don't forget, when you come to the last step, that if the paving adjoins grass, it should finish just a little below the grass level for easy mowing.

Stepping stones

If you turn back to pages 10 & 11, you'll see from the plan of the Barnsdale garden, that it was desirable to have a link between the semi-circular paved area, and the circular scree garden.

I decided against a continuous path, because it would have looked too hard and formal. Stepping stones, with planting in between were an ideal solution. They form an effective liaison between the rather more formal character of the paved area, and the informality of the scree garden.

Stepping stones are also useful where a path is needed in the lawn, but you don't want to break the area into two pieces with a continuous line. The fact that there is grass between the stepping stones, still leaves the impression of a continuous sweep of grass, rather than two strips. Thus, the lawn looks bigger and the garden less bitty. It is very important in small gardens, to avoid breaking the design up into strips.

The first thing to do, is to set out the slabs on the surface. Have a good look at them to ensure that they look right, and also walk down them to make sure that they are spaced in a way that makes walking comfortable.

I don't go to all the trouble of making a concrete base for stepping stones. Firstly, they don't get the use that paving would, so they are less likely to sink, and even if they do, a little change in level is acceptable. But the main reason for setting them on sand in this case was that I wanted to allow plant roots to grow underneath them. There are several plants, ideal for growing between stepping stones, that require a cool, moist root-run, which is just what they get underneath a paving slab.

So, once the position of the slabs was ascertained, I simply lifted them one by one, cut out beneath them, and laid them on a bed of soft sand. It's a bit of a fiddle getting them at the right level, but you soon get the hang of it.

If the stones are set in grass, the turf is cut round the stone with a half-moon edging tool, and then removed. A little soil is then taken out and replaced with soft sand. When tapped down firmly, the stones should finish about $\frac{1}{2}$ in. (13 mm.) below the level of the turf for easy mowing.

Plants for paving and walls

However attractive the paving or walling stone selected, and however well it is laid, there is no doubt that stone always tends to look a bit hard. Large areas of paving and walling can be softened and made very attractive by planting, both between the paving slabs and in special pockets left in the slabs, or between walling stones. I have never ceased to be amazed at the small amount of soil needed by many alpine and rock plants to survive and indeed, flourish.

I have already pointed out that I left some holes in the paving for larger plants, and I also brushed soil in between the cracks in the slabs to take smaller, less demanding subjects. To me, gardens are all about plants and I can't resist growing them wherever they will survive. Now they are beginning to get established, they look really attractive all the year round, with various colours and textures of foliage. They also seem to want to flower until they burst, so even the paved area can be a riot of colour at certain times of the year.

Obviously, one must be careful about choosing the right

plants, and the right place to put them. It's no good planting large or tender subjects in a part of the paved area that is to be used regularly. Certainly there are some subjects that will put up with a bit of wear and tear, but generally, I feel that it's better to keep the main walkways and the sitting-out area free from planting. Even though they seem to suffer little damage, I hate to tread on plants – even those that will put up with it. However, I know I'm going to find it difficult to pull out plants that stray into the wrong place, as many of these paving plants will, so I suppose I shall get taken over eventually.

If you brush soil into the cracks between the paving, there will inevitably be trouble with weeds. Seeds are bound to germinate in the spaces, and they, I must admit, cause problems. If there are cultivated plants close by, it is impossible to use weed-killers, so the only alternative is to weed by hand until the cultivated plants take over. With an old kitchen knife, it's not an unpleasant job.

The one other disadvantage I have found with planting a paved area, is that the foliage does tend to collect fallen leaves in the autumn. If you are a passionately tidy gardener, this could prove irksome. I'm not, and I'm convinced that the chore of a bit of weeding between slabs, and picking up leaves by hand is well-compensated for by the extra colour and interest provided by planting.

A bed for acid-lovers

If your paved area is large, it may well be possible to include a bigger space in it somewhere for planting larger conifers, heathers, and flowering shrubs. If your soil is on the limey side, this is the ideal spot for making a special ericaceous border. All you have to do is to dig out fairly deeply – about 3 ft (1 m.) will be plenty – and line the bottom of the hole with some strong polythene. Pierce a few holes in the sheeting to provide drainage, and fill the space with a compost consisting of 7 parts of lime-free soil, 3 parts of peat and 2 parts of coarse grit. Here you can plant acid-loving subjects that will not do well in other parts of the garden.

Obviously, it would be folly to use plants that will grow too vigorously. Not only will they take up too much room, but they will eventually root through the holes in the polythene, into the alkaline soil, more or less committing suicide.

But there are plenty of smaller rhododendrons, heathers, daboecias etc. that will make a fine show.

Heathers

Heathers will provide a show of colour from both flowers and foliage, the whole year round. There is more information on varieties in the chapter on the heather and conifer border. For this sort of planting, low-growing varieties should be used, of which there is a very wide choice.

Erica carnea varieties flower throughout the winter and early spring and are lime-tolerant. There are several with coloured foliage to add interest even when they are not in flower. *Erica darleyensis* varieties are also winter-flowering, and ideal ground-coverers. *Erica tetralix*, the 'Cross-leaved Heath', flowers from June to October, and the colours vary from white, through pink to red. *Erica vagans*, the 'Cornish Heath', produces long sprays of foliage from July to October, ranging from white to rose-pink. Some varieties have the bonus of coloured foliage.

Calluna, the various varieties of 'Ling' (*Calluna vulgaris*), flower from July to November, and there are many with highly attractive foliage.

Daboecia, the 'Bell Heathers', are closely related to the Ericas, and all are suitable. Unless you live in a very sheltered spot, choose one of the varieties of *D. cantabrica*, the 'Connemara Heath'. These flower from June to November and come in a range of colours from white to purple.

Rhododendron – there is an enormous variety of rhododendron species and hybrids, several of which are suitable for planting in paved beds. However, some types will grow very large indeed, and these must be avoided. The final choice will depend upon the size of the bed. If it is small, stick to dwarf varieties like *R. calostrotum*, of which I think the best is the red form 'Gigha'. No paved area should be without *R. impeditum* which has grey-green foliage and masses of tiny blue flowers.

Heathers spill over onto the paved area

Of the small hybrids, I am particularly fond of 'Blue Tit', which forms a perfectly rounded bush, covered in blue flowers during May and June. 'Carmen' flowers at much the same time, with a profusion of dark crimson flowers, while 'Chikor' sports yellow flowers also during May and June. But perhaps my all-time favourite dwarf rhododendron is 'Elizabeth'. The masses of dark-red trumpets during April make it a must. For the larger bed, the R. *yakushimanum* hybrids are not to be missed. They grow slowly, and produce a profusion of flowers of various colours, offset by shining, evergreen foliage.

Of course, there are many more varieties available in nurseries and garden centres. They flower in spring, so it's well worth a visit to see them for yourself.

Plants for small holes in paving

Having left holes at strategic positions out of the way of chairs, tables and your size nine boots, the choice of plants must depend upon the same criterion. They must not spread so far that they become a nuisance.

A plant, for example, like *Juniperus media 'Pfitzeriana'*, looks very much like a prostrate conifer when it's young and indeed, it is often sold as such. In fact, it will form in only a few years an enormous mountain of foliage, spreading over several yards and growing eight or nine feet tall. Definitely not for the small patio. There is a multitude of conifers, small shrubs, alpine and rock-garden plants that will fill the planting hole and spread a little way over the paving without becoming a liability.

Conifers

While it is possible to plant small, upright conifers like *Juniperus communis 'Compressa'* in paving, I feel that, planted alone they tend to look like the proverbial sore-thumb. They really need company. So, I have stuck to prostrate growers that will hug the paving and spread out to form a compact carpet of foliage.

Juniperus species are undoubtedly the most useful of prostrate conifers. There are several varieties ideal for planting in paving, and a few that can be used to hang down over a wall to very good effect.

Juniperus communis 'Depressa Aurea' is one of the most decorative of shrubs for planting in paving. It will spread to upwards of 10 ft (3 m.) in good conditions, but it is relatively slow growing and will stand a lot of pruning back. In the summer its foliage is a glorious golden yellow, which changes to deep bronze in winter. *Juniperus communis 'Repanda'* is more vigorous and perhaps not so decorative. Its green foliage also turns bronze in winter. But this one is really only for the larger paved area.

Juniperus conferta, the 'Shore Juniper', is an ideal subject for

Juniperus conferta

growing on the top of walls. It will grow to 'tip' over the edge, where it continues to hug the wall in a most attractive way. The foliage is bright, apple-green. *Juniperus horizontalis* is ideal for covering walls in the same way, and can be used in larger areas of paving to good effect. One of the best is *J. c. 'Montana'*, which produces long branches of dense, silver-blue foliage. *Juniperus procumbens 'Nana'* grows very tight to the ground, forming a mat of bright, apple-green foliage. *Juniperus sargentii 'Compacta'* is a slow growing, deep green variety, suited to the smaller patio.

Rockery and alpine plants

There are literally hundreds of rock garden and alpine plants that are well suited to growing in paving pockets. Many will also grow in crevices between walling stones or in the cracks between the paving. I have limited myself to listing just a few of my favourites that I have planted at Barnsdale. They require very little attention, though I have found that dead-heading the larger plants does a lot to increase their flowering period.

Hypericum species produce orange or red buds, opening to quite large, bright yellow flowers, which continue to come throughout the summer. *H. olympicum* is one of the most beautiful with slender upright stems terminating in large, golden-yellow flowers. The variety *'Citrinum'* is perhaps even lovelier, with much paler, pastel-yellow flowers. Hardier and shorter, is *H. polyphillum*, which bears a profusion of golden-yellow flowers marked with conspicuous scarlet. But perhaps the best of them all, is *H. reptans*. This is very prostrate in habit, and is excellent for planting near the edge of a wall, where it will hang over, hugging the stonework.

Campanulas are everybody's favourite, and I am no exception. Common of course they are, and with very good reason. They produce a mass of blue, bell-shaped flowers all summer long and are amongst the easiest to grow. They may need a little water during hot, dry spells, but other than this they will grow in

Hypericum olympicum

Campanula cochlearifolia

shade or sun, and are the most accommodating of plants. There are well over a hundred species which are suitable for paving or walls, so I will confine myself to those I have planted. *C. cochlearifolia* often sold as *C. pusilla* is without doubt the best-tempered of the lot. It never fails to produce hundreds of nodding bells in shades of blue or white. *C. garganica* produces long-flowering sprays, covered with masses of small, starry flowers in late summer. It is ideal in crevices of the wall, or in the paving. *C. × haylodgensis 'Flore Pleno'* is ideally suited to small spaces, and will grow well in wall crevices. It is one of the few double-flowered campanulas.

Potentillas are a large genus of shrubby and herbaceous plants, some of which are prostrate and good for this sort of situation. Best of all is *P. nitida* which has silvery foliage and large flowers varying from rose-pink to white.

Thymus species are attractive in flower and foliage and have the added advantage of a strong, but very pleasant perfume which is released when the plant is brushed. *Thymus serpyllum* is a common, prostrate species with many varieties in cultivation. The colours available range from white, through pink to deep red. *Thymus × citriodorus* as the name suggests is lemon-scented. There are two varieties generally offered, both worth having. *T. c. 'Aureus'* has bright golden foliage that looks especially good in winter, while *T. c. 'Silver Queen'*, has silver foliage.

Thymus serpyllum

Pulsatilla vulgaris, the 'Pasque Flower' is still often sold as *Anemone pulsatilla*. Though a native wild-flower in England, the cultivated forms make bushier plants and carry more flowers, ranging in variety from white through red to deep purple.

Polygonum may be a name that fills many gardeners with horror, since it is generally associated with the rampant and not very attractive climber. There are a couple of species of mat-forming plants that provide welcome flowers in the autumn. The best, in my opinion, is *P. vacciniifolium*, which produces slender, erect spikes of red flowers over a long period.

Phlox subulata forms wide mats of tufted foliage, covered in April and May with a wealth of flowers. There are several varieties in cultivation varying from white, through pink to magenta/crimson.

Dianthus alpinus forms a mat of deep green, with large, attractive flowers ranging from deep rose-pink to white. *D. neglectus* is perhaps even more beautiful, forming matted, grass-like clumps, out of which rise stems of deep pink, often with a blue centre.

Cytisus kewensis is an excellent, prostrate broom, especially suited to planting on the edge of a wall. In early summer, it produces cascades of creamy-white flowers.

Above (top to bottom): *Pulsatilla vulgaris; Phlox subulata; Dianthus alpinus*

Left: *Cytisus kewensis*

Plants for crevices

Again, there are hundreds of rock and alpine plants suitable for growing in the small cracks between paving stones and in holes left in the wall. Some will inevitably spread and become invasive, though on paving, constant pedestrian traffic will help to keep them under control. They need very little soil for survival, and require no maintenance at all.

Some such plants are too well known to require description. But nonetheless, such 'peasants' as *Aubretias, Arabis* and *Alyssum saxatile* are not to be despised. They are popular because they produce a positive riot of colour and are the easiest plants in the world to grow. They can easily be raised from seed, so it's not a bad idea to use some in the first instance, and to replace them with choicer subjects as the fancy takes you, and as the 'new-garden budget' becomes a little less strained. The popular 'Three S's' – the *Saxifrages, Sedums* and *Sempervivums* are enough in themselves to cover a paved area with flower. There are hundreds of species, many of which will grow well almost anywhere. We have all seen our native 'House-leeks' (*Sempervivum*) and 'Stonecrops' (*Saxifraga*) growing on roofs and in walls with little or no apparent source of sustenance. They flourish and seem to flower

The 'peasant' *Aubretia*

Alyssum saxatile

for ever. About the only requirement they insist upon is good drainage, and they are bound to get that in paving or on a wall.

Sisyrinchium is a genus of invasive, iris-like plants. On the rock garden, they can become a nuisance, because their creeping roots spread everywhere. In paving, that is an ideal attribute, and they will not become problematic. *S. angustifolium* produces dense tufts of leaves and bright blue flowers, while *S. brachypus* has much the same habit, but flowers of clear, bright yellow. One of the very best is *S. filifolium* with delicate, pendant flowers of white, delicately veined with purple.

Mentha requienii is a minute plant, quite unlike the culinary mint we all know, yet of the same family. Its tiny, peppermint-

Above: *Nierembergia repens*

Right: *Erinus alpinus* contrasts well with a *Hebe*

scented leaves form a dense film of green over paving stones and it produces masses of small purple flowers in summer. *Acaena microphylla* is grown mainly as a foliage plant. It forms large mats of bronze-green with deep scarlet burrs in late summer.

Cotula squalida is another foliage plant with deep-cut, bronze-tinged leaves but inconspicuous flowers.

Erinus alpinus is especially suited to cracks and crevices in walls. There is a lilac and a white form while 'Dr Hanelle' and 'Mrs Charles Boyle' are both pink.

Gypsophylla repens is an excellent plant for planting at the top of a wall to hang down over the front. It has grey-green leaves and myriads of flowers varying according to the form, from white to clear pink.

Raoulia australis forms flat carpets of tiny silvery leaves and bears sulphur yellow flowers in summer. It may succumb to wet weather in winter. *R. glabra* is easier to grow, bearing white flowers on a carpet of green foliage.

Nierembergia repens (sometimes called *N. rivularis*), forms a dense mat of upright, dark green leaves, and bears a profusion of white, cup-shaped flowers.

The plants I have listed here all have different growth rates. As they grow, it soon becomes obvious which are the brash young hustlers and which the shy little flowers. Some refereeing is going to be needed to keep the more invasive under control so as to give the others a chance.

LAWNS

An area of grass is one of the basic constituents of most British gardens and Barnsdale is no exception. We in Britain, are lucky to have just about the best climate in the world for producing good lawns, and this is perhaps, one of the reasons why they are almost obligatory.

But, apart from that, they serve to link the planting and other features together to give the whole garden a sense of continuity and space. The rich green of a good lawn provides the ideal foreground to set off the more colourful borders beyond and, well-maintained, it is one of the features of the garden that will look good all the year round.

At Barnsdale, the lawn area was designed to sweep right round the cottage without a break. For me, this is a basic, and very important design principle. Once you start to cut a lawn up with paths, the sense of space is lost and the whole scheme begins to look 'bitty' and disconnected.

A well-kept lawn makes a perfect foreground for the mixed border

From a purely practical viewpoint, long sweeps of grass are much easier to maintain. If borders are designed in long, gentle curves and fiddly corners are kept to a minimum, you'll be able to run the mower round without even a pause for breath. For the same reason, where the grass joins paving, it should be made to stand a little above it, so that the mower can pass right over and cut up to the edge with no difficulty.

At Barnsdale, the lawn was to be purely decorative, so I was quite happy to retain the natural slopes. But, if I had wanted to use it for some specific purpose, I might well have decided to spend a little time and trouble over levelling. If, for example, you want to use it for leisure activities – croquet, clock golf or cricket for the kids for example, you may prefer to sacrifice the interest of a 'landscaped' lawn so that it can be used effectively.

But for the purely decorative garden, I think we often worry too much about getting a perfect level. In just the same way that the borders of an informal garden should be curved, rather than straight, so the levels should also be somewhat indiscriminate. Slopes and gentle undulations give a much more natural, less contrived look. The only criterion should be whether or not you can mow it without difficulty. So obviously, you'll need to eliminate small local bumps and hollows, and very sharp slopes.

Levelling

When the initial cultivations and soil improvements are completed (see the chapter on Land clearance), the lawn area should be marked out with canes and then consolidated and levelled.

It's worth taking a bit of time and trouble over this stage because, if the lawn is unlevel due to either bad initial levelling or subsequent sinkage, it is very difficult to rectify.

Start by going over the whole area, roughly levelling with the back of a fork. You will have to choose the right time and weather conditions for this, especially if your soil is on the heavy side. The golden rule is that if the soil sticks to your boots, keep off. Treading all over sticky, wet soil will ruin the structure and heavy soils especially will set like concrete when they dry out.

The object of the initial levelling is just to fill up larger hollows and remove high spots. If the levels are very bad, you may well find that you have to move large amounts of soil with the wheelbarrow, and cart them to a low spot somewhere else. If you do need to do this, try to get hold of some boards to wheel on. Scaffold boards are ideal, and can be hired quite cheaply. They will make the job much easier and again, they will prevent damage to the soil structure.

After roughly levelling, when you are satisfied that the contour of the land is more or less as you want it, the soil must be consolidated. There really is only one way to do it, and that, I'm afraid, is the hard way. There is no substitute for treading over

1 Go over the whole area, roughly levelling it with the back of a fork

the whole area with your weight on your heels, making sure that you cover every square inch. Rolling it will *not* do. All that does is to push down the high areas, and leave the hollows untouched, and that simply makes the matter worse.

Start in one corner, and shuffle round like a kid playing trains (it's wise to try to time this job for when the neighbours are out!). Work right the way round systematically, so that you cover every bit of the land, and pay special attention to soil butting onto paving. This must be really firm to prevent sinkage and avoid later damage to the mower.

Before final levelling, fertiliser should be applied, to give the new grass a good start in life. I use the same fertiliser, whether I am laying turf or seeding. In the spring or summer, I have got the best results from an application of Growmore at about 3 oz per sq.yd (90 gm per sq.m.). In the autumn, the extra nitrogen could make the young grass grow a little too lush and soft, and it could suffer if the winter is hard. Bonemeal is better at that time, and it should be applied at the same rate.

Spreading fertiliser at the correct rate is a problem – if you buy it from a garden centre, you may be able to borrow or hire a special distributor. Only if your lawn is big do I think it's worth while buying one. After the initial sowing, you'll only use it two or three times a year, but it does save a lot of work, and it applies the fertiliser very accurately. You could well recoup the cost over several years by ensuring that you don't put on too much.

The next best bet, after the classy wheeled jobs, is a small 'shaker'. This is a trough-shaped box made of corrugated plastic. You simply fill it up with fertiliser and shake it over the area to be grassed. They do a surprisingly good job. It is possible to spread the fertiliser fairly accurately by hand, and this is what I did at Barnsdale. I simply weighed out 3 oz (85 gm) on the kitchen scales, marked out a square yard, and spread it evenly just to see what it looked like on the ground. I found that a handful was

2 Consolidate the soil by treading over the whole area with your weight on your heels

3 Take special care on soil adjacent to paved areas to avoid sinking

4 About a fortnight before turfing, apply a light dressing of general fertiliser

5 Rake the area down to a fine tilth and a good level, eliminating bumps and hollows

6 Stand back from time to time and squint across the surface to check the levels

near enough an ounce, and once I got going, it was fairly easy to judge by looking at the fertiliser on the ground. Certainly there is a fair margin of error, and my grass seems to thrive on it.

The final levelling will work the fertiliser into the top couple of inches and provide the fine tilth necessary for sowing seed or laying turf. It is often said that it is not necessary to prepare soil for turf to the same standards of level and tilth needed for seed sowing. I simply can't agree. There is no doubt in my mind that turf will go down much easier and, more importantly, to a much better level, if the soil underneath it is fine, firm and level. So I prepare for both methods in exactly the same way.

The secret of raking soil absolutely level, is to take short strokes and to keep the head of the rake fairly flat to the ground. Don't reach out as far as you can with the rake and pull the soil towards you. That tends to create ridges at the far end of the stroke. Work with the rake no more than a foot or two in front of you, and you'll find it easier to level and easier to see when the correct level has been achieved.

You should, after a little practice, be able to judge the level by eye. If you find it difficult, stretch a tight line across the land you have raked down, about 1 in (2.5 cm) above the soil level. Then stand back and squint across the soil, with your head as near ground level as you can get it. By comparing the level of the land with the line, the high or low spots will be easily seen.

You may find, especially on light soil, that you rake up a lot of stones. For turf, they don't matter a great deal, since the turf itself will hold them down in the soil. But if you have decided to use seed, the best bet is to remove them completely. In fact, you'll find that, after sowing, more stones will work their way to the surface. The bigger ones will have to be picked off by hand before mowing, but, once the grass gets a hold it will keep them down below the surface.

The grass next to a paved area should finish about 1 in. (2.5 cm.)

above it. If you are using turf, there is little problem. Simply rake the soil over onto the paving, and then push it back with the back of the rake. The thickness of the turf will help raise it, and, as soon as it roots through, it will hold the edge solid.

But, if you are sowing the lawn, you'll have to take steps to ensure a good edge between the grass and the paving. The best way is to put some fairly wide, 1 in. (2.5 cm.) thick boards on the edge of the paving, and to draw the soil up to those. A few bricks on the boards will hold them in place until the seed has made enough roots to hold the edge firm.

Turf or seed

The choice between turf or seed depends upon many factors. Both have their advantages and disadvantages and you must weigh them up, one against the other, to decide which best suits your particular situation.

Seed has the advantage first and foremost, that it is cheaper. Even the best seed should cost less than half the price of turf but I feel that a good lawn is so important that it is better to risk the apoplexy of the bank manager than to skimp on the job.

The main advantage with seed as I see it, is that you'll get just the sort of grass you want. If you need a lawn that will take a bit of wear, you can get the appropriate mixture. If the lawn will be shaded by trees, there's a grass seed to suit, or, if you want the finest of bowling-green finishes, there's a mixture for you too.

Turf, on the other hand, is a bit of an unknown quantity. It is often difficult to see a sample before you buy, and some turf-merchants' descriptions are somewhat less than accurate. At best, you will get weed-treated parkland turf. Some is pretty good, though most has a certain amount of weed and coarse grass in it, though this can generally be cut out as you use it. At worst, you will be blessed with untreated cow pasture. I have even seen it complete with cow-pads!

But, the great advantage with turf, is that you get an instant result. Immediately after laying, your lawn will at least look like a lawn, and it will be usable after about two months. A seeded lawn will take considerably longer than that.

After weighing the pros and cons, I decided on seed. I was not in any great hurry and the final quality of the grass was more important to me than either cost or time.

Buying seed

Gone are the days when you could buy seed mixtures made up especially for you in the shop, but there are plenty of good, prepacked mixtures to suit most situations. The type of mixture to choose depends upon three factors. Firstly, the site is import-ant, the main factor being whether the lawn is in shade or full sun. There are species of grass that will thrive in shady situations, and these are included in proprietary mixtures recommended for shaded sites.

For the majority of gardens, the two main considerations are the wear and tear the lawn will have to withstand and the amount of work you are prepared to put into maintenance.

If you have children, you will just have to learn to live with them playing football on your prized lawn, so it is only realistic to use a mixture that will put up with a lot of wear. There are plenty of really tough grasses about, and these are included in proprietary 'hard-wearing' mixtures.

But the amount of time and trouble you are prepared to spend on your lawn is crucial. There is absolutely no point in buying a first-class, fine mixture without rye-grass, unless you are prepared to cut it at least twice, and preferably three times a week. Cut once a week or less, and used normally, the coarser grasses will take over in no time, and the extra cost of fine grasses will be lost. Conversely, I have seen the finest of fine lawns developed from what was originally nothing but cow-pasture. But that takes daily mowing and plenty of fertiliser, weedkiller and water.

In the past, all the research done on grass species, was carried out with cattle grazing in mind. As a result of that, several strains of perennial rye-grass were developed, that were short, leafy and slow to run to seed. Now the plant breeders have gone one better, and there are now several strains of PRG developed specifically for lawns. They are shorter and leafier than ever before, and have the added advantage of deep roots, making the lawn very resistant to drought. They produce an excellent lawn, that will require no more than weekly cutting, and normal care.

Since I did not wish to be tied to cutting my lawn three times a week, I chose one of these. The strain is called 'Hunter' and it is marketed by Hursts Seeds. This one, in fact, is not a mixture, but just this one variety. There are others that use much the same sort of strain in a mixture, and one of these would be ideal for a garden where the conditions of light are varied.

It is generally recommended by seedsmen that grass seed should be sown at 2 oz per sq.yd (60 gm per sq.m.), but I have proved this to be an unnecessarily high rate. On my lawn at Barnsdale, I sowed half at the recommended rate, and the other half at only 1 oz per sq.yd (30 gm per sq.m.). Within just eight weeks of germination, it was impossible to tell the difference.

So, to order the required quantity, all you have to do is to measure up the area in square yards and that will be the amount of seed you need in ounces.

Sowing
Lawn seed can be sown more or less from April to October, but the best times are doubtless late April or late August. Of the

two, I prefer August. Despite what the British Tourist Board would have you believe, there is generally enough rain at that time to give good germination and growth, and the soil is at its warmest. By winter, the grass will be well enough established to withstand any amount of cold and wet.

In April, dry spells are quite on the cards, and it is far from unknown to have a good sprinkling of snow. But, one can't, of course, always wait any longer. I couldn't, so I sowed the Barnsdale lawn in April. If you sow later than this, the risk of a dry spell is increased, so you must be prepared to water. Ideally, water the soil with a lawn sprinkler a day *before* sowing. That way the soil should hold enough moisture for germination, after which more can be applied. If you water before the seed has germinated, you risk washing it into the hollows, resulting in patchy germination.

If you have invested in a fertiliser distributor, the seed can be spread with that. Adjust the machine so that not too much seed comes out, and go over the area two or three times to get an even application.

Sowing by hand has, in my opinion, been made over-complicated. All that measuring out with garden lines and 3 ft (1 m.) canes is not really necessary. A handful of seed will contain just about 1 oz (28gm), and one good pace is near enough a yard. I sowed my lawn by this rule of thumb method, and it all came up very evenly.

If you feel worried about doing it this way, just mark out one square yard in the normal way, and sow a weighed amount. Then you'll be able to see roughly how much you should be putting down. There really is no need to be that accurate.

After sowing, the seed must be raked in. Now it is even more important to keep the head of the rake fairly flat with the ground, to avoid spoiling the levels. Aim to cover about half the seed with soil. There is no need to roll afterwards.

1 To check the amount of seed needed, set two lines 3 ft (1 m.) apart

2 With a 3 ft (1 m.) cane, measure out and mark a line in the soil

3 Scatter the seed evenly over the marked area. There should be no need to mark out the whole lawn

4 After sowing, rake the seed into the surface, aiming to cover about half

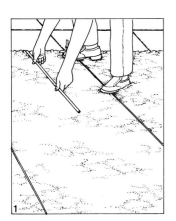
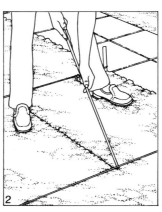

Most grass seed these days is treated with a bird deterrent. I reckon it's like adding parsley sauce to fish. Birds will still have a field day on your new lawn, filling themselves up with as much as they can eat, while you pick up the bill. So, it is important to take steps to discourage them. It is no easy matter to deter birds. I have tried all sorts of methods, including scarecrows and many of the proprietary bird scaring devices. None are really one hundred per cent effective. The best way, is to put a series of pegs around the new lawn, and to stretch black cotton between them. I have never seen a bird get trapped in the cotton, but it seems to give them a sense of insecurity, and they fly off in search of someone else's new lawn. I actually have two killer cats who, I'm sure have a little Mafia blood in them. They never seem to actually catch their feathered quarry, but they run an effective protection racket.

Aftercare

Once the seed has germinated, make sure it never goes short of water. The roots will be quite small at first, so the watering regime should be little and often, rather than infrequent soakings.

When it has reached about 2 in. (5 cm.) high, it is ready for its first cut. Before doing so, walk over the whole area, bucket in hand, and pick off any stones that may damage the mower blades.

Set the front roller on the mower, as low as it will go, for the first cut, raising the blades to their highest point. For the second and subsequent mowings, it can be raised gradually, until finally the blades are leaving the grass about 1 in. (2.5 cm.) long.

Turfing

Buying turf can be a bit of a tricky business. It's a bit like taking on a wife really. You need a bit of vigilance, a bit of common-sense, and a lot of luck.

There are, of course, a fair few good, reliable turf merchants about. There is also a good sprinkling of 'cowboys'. The problem is to be able to differentiate between the two. Good turf should have been cut regularly, rolled and weed treated for a season before it is sold. It should have plenty of 'fibre' in it to help it hold together, and it should be evenly cut.

Unfortunately, it is often impossible to see it before buying.

If you can get out to see it in the field, or look at some they have delivered locally, so much the better. If not, tell the merchant exactly your requirements, and suggest to him that you may not accept delivery if the turf is not up to standard.

It is a false economy to buy the cheapest turf advertised. If you want good stuff, you'll have to pay for it. You must also never expect perfection from parkland turf. There are bound to be the odd few weeds and coarse grasses in it, but these can

easily be removed either during laying, or by good management afterwards.

If you are quite set on the very best, it is now possible to buy specially raised turf. This consists of a plastic mesh, either covered with compost or floated on a liquid nutrient solution, and then sown with grass seed. The quality is excellent, but of course, the price is considerably higher.

At Barnsdale, I chose a good quality parkland turf that had, so I was assured, been weed-treated, cut and rolled for a full season. It cost half as much again as the cheapest advertised, but was well worth it in the end.

Turf is ordered in square yards (or metres), so it is only necessary to measure up the area and add a little for wastage. Don't order, though, until you are quite ready. When stacked in rolls, turf will quickly go yellow, especially in the summer months.

Laying turf

Turf can be laid at any time of the year, except when there is frost in the ground, or the soil is too wet. At these times, it is unlikely that the merchants will be able to cut it anyway. However, if you intend to lay it during the hotter, drier summer months, you *must* be prepared to water regularly. Once turves begin to dry out, they shrink, leaving large, ugly gaps between. When the rains do come, they will often root into the soil before they have a chance to expand again, and you will be left with those gaps.

Remember that until the grass roots through, it has no means of taking up water from the soil. All it has to survive on, is the moisture within the turf itself. So, watering should be little and often. In hot weather, you must be prepared to keep the sprinkler on the new grass all day, moving it about every hour, for at least a week.

All in all, if it is at all convenient, it is safer to lay it when wet weather can be expected. With the vagaries of the British weather in mind, I suppose that could be considered pretty useless advice. But the months of April or September are reasonably safe.

Soil preparation is exactly the same as that described for seeding. Don't try to get away with anything less of a tilth. It is much easier to lay turf well on a good, even surface, and it will also ensure that all the roots are in close contact with the soil.

Before starting to lay, make sure you have plenty of good, wide boards handy. Scaffold boards are ideal. At no stage should you walk either on the turf you have laid, or on the soil you have so carefully prepared, so it is necessary to work off boards all the time.

If there is one straight edge to the lawn, that's the place to start. Lay out the first row and pull the ends of the turves into each other using the back of the rake. Now tap them down all

1 Lay out the first turf, preferably starting on a side with a straight edge

2 Pull the turf tight into the paving edge with the back of the rake

3 The edging turves are best laid out first to give a good, sweeping curve

4 Tap the first row of turves down gently using the back of the rake

over making sure that the surface is flat. There is no need, if your preparation has been good, to hammer the turves down – with evenly-cut turf and a level base, the object of the exercise is simply to ensure that all the roots are in close contact with the soil, and to take out any little local humps and bumps.

Before you lay the next row, lay out the turves that will make the edge of the lawn, treading on the soil that will eventually form the borders. That will have to be dug afterwards in any case. If you lay the edges first, you can easily see the correct line of curved borders.

Put a row of scaffold boards on the first turves you laid, and then the second row can be put down in exactly the same way, pulling it into the first row with the back of the rake.

At the end of the row, simply lay the last turf over the top of the edging turf, and cut off the excess with a knife.

Unless the turf is of a very high standard indeed, you are bound to come across some with holes in them, or pieces missing from the edges. All you have to do here, is to tear off a scrap

5 Lay wide boards onto the turf and move them forward as work progresses

6 Lay the second row, and again, pull it into the first row with the back of the rake

7 At the ends, lay the last turf over the edging turf and cut off the excess

8 When digging the borders, avoid digging too close to the turf until it has rooted

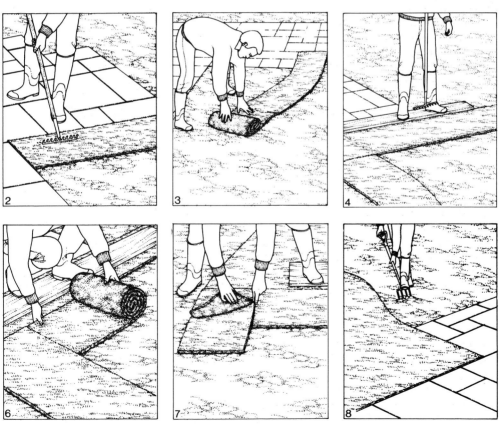
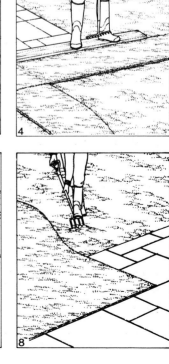

of turf from one of the odd pieces you will accumulate as you go along, and stuff it into the hole. It will root through just the same and become quite unnoticeable.

Once the whole area is laid, remove the boards, and keep off for a week or so. As I mentioned before, there is likely to be a need for water in the early stages, but this is all the aftercare the lawn will need until it is ready for its first cut. There is no need to roll it, and there shouldn't be any necessity to brush soil into the cracks between the turves, as some authorities suggest. If you've laid it properly and keep applying the water, there won't *be* any cracks.

At first, the grass will look a bit sorry for itself. Even with regular watering, it always tends to lie flat and look a little sad. As soon as it roots through, it will quickly shake off its blues, green up and start to stand up straight. In the spring and summer, this normally takes about a week to ten days, and a little longer in the winter.

Once it does this, stop watering, in preparation for the first cut. After all that water, the ground underneath the turf is bound to be a bit soft. Walking on it will almost certainly leave footmarks, so you must control your enthusiasm for a day or two. Test it gently before putting your whole weight on it, and even then, tread carefully.

As with seeded lawns, the first cut should be with the mower blades set as high as possible. They should be lowered at each successive cut, to finish at about 1 in. (2.5 cm.) or so. There is nothing worse for any lawn, and particularly a new one, than leaving the grass to grow long, and then cutting it short.

Aftercare

No plant in our gardens is treated quite so badly as we treat our grass. And none is expected to perform so well, despite our maltreatment. So in order to compensate for our conscience and to get the best results, we must lavish a little care. After all, we tread all over it every day, we prune it back hard at least once a week, our kids play on it, and our dogs and cats commit quite unmentionable sins on it, and still it comes up smiling, so it deserves a treat every so often.

Mowing

Cutting the grass is the most regular job in the garden and the most important for good lawns. The amount of cutting will determine the quality of the grass to a large extent. This is because fine grasses thrive on regular trimming, while the coarser-leaved varieties hate it. Eventually, if a rough lawn is cut every day, the coarse grasses will die out, and finer species will take their place. It's not *quite* as simple as that, but in principle it is certainly true.

The lawn at Barnsdale is cut at least once a week in the growing season

In order to give those fine grasses the best chance, conditions must be made just right for them to flourish, so the lawn must also be fertilised and watered, mulched and aerated.

The type of mower also makes a big difference to the quality of the grass. Not only must it be cut regularly, but that cutting must also be as even as possible. When choosing a mower for a fine lawn, buy one with as many cutting blades in the cylinder as possible. They will give a much more even cut and a finer lawn.

Rotary mowers are not really suitable for fine grasses, though if you only intend to cut the grass once a week, they will do well.

As I have said, the lawns at Barnsdale were not intended to be the finest possible and like most gardeners I have compromised. I have a medium/fine lawn which is green and relatively weed-free, but tough enough to take a bit of wear and tear. I started with a fine-leaved rye-grass and I now cut it at least once a week, and twice when it is growing really strongly.

I also feel that it is important to cut in opposite directions on each successive mowing. If grass is laid down in one direction on the first mowing, it is picked up and cut cleanly next time. Now it would obviously be impossible to do this if you mowed straight up and down the lawn. Once the 'stripes' have disappeared, you can never tell which way you mowed last time. So, I cut diagonally across the lawn each time. Before cutting I put a marker in the border at the corner where I started, and the next time, I start in the opposite corner and mow across the previous direction.

Great controversy rages over whether to mow with the box on, or to leave the cuttings on the lawn. I'm not so sure that many of the arguments are that scientific. Me, I just use my common sense. In fact, I do both.

The arguments are generally put forward by the mower manufacturers. Those who make machines that pick up the grass claim that leaving the cuttings on makes a thick 'thatch' of dead grass, preventing water and air reaching the roots. They produce solid, scientific evidence to support their theories. While the anti-box faction will suggest equally scientific-sounding arguments to support leaving the cuttings. They say that they eventually work into the soil to improve the structure and add nutrients. I think they are both right – and wrong.

I have two distinct types of soil on my lawn at Barnsdale. Part of it lies on excellent soil, rich in organic matter and the grass there grows strongly and quickly. But elsewhere the soil is thinner and sandier and there is little organic matter to hold water and nutrients. So, when the grass is growing strongly on the good soil, I remove the cuttings, but on the thin patch, I always leave them on to work back into the soil. The system seems to work very well. I think a lot depends upon the rest of the maintenance programme.

Underneath the trees at Barnsdale, I also have a stretch of rougher grass. Fine grass needs lots of sunlight to grow well, so it's necessary to leave grass in shady places, a little longer. I cut mine no more than once a month, and when I do, I leave it about 4 in. (10 cm.) long. This area is cut with a rotary mower, but because the grass is long when it's cut, I rake off the grass just to tidy it up.

The long grass is also naturalised with daffodils and crocuses. Since it is essential to leave the foliage of bulbs to die down naturally, I never start cutting until about the end of May.

Feeding

Fertiliser is just as important for grass as for any other plant. It is, perhaps, even more important in fact, because such a lot of plant nutrients are removed every week with the cuttings. I feed with a straightforward lawn fertiliser, put on with a wheeled spreader. It is an expensive item I know, but it makes all the difference to the lawn. A cheaper way to do it is with a liquid feed, but since the fertiliser is more quickly dispersed in this form, more applications are necessary.

I start feeding when the grasses are growing vigorously in the spring. That's generally about the end of April here. Then I put on another application in June, followed by a dressing of autumn lawn food in September.

Lawn fertilisers are very high in nitrogen, which is why they give such a green colour after application. But this high nitrogen content can make them dangerous if they are put on at too heavy a rate. I have seen grass badly scorched by applying too much. It is therefore essential to apply no more than the recommended dose. Some garden centres will lend out a fertiliser spreader when you buy the feed, and I think it's worth searching out those who do. It saves an awful lot of work and even more worry.

A cheaper fertiliser to use would be Growmore. It will supply the essential nutrients, but since its nitrogen content is lower, it will not give that immediate greening effect.

Watering

After feeding, it is important to water the grass if rain doesn't fall within a couple of days. Otherwise, scorching could again occur. Because grass is such a leafy plant, and because of the constant removal of water with the cuttings, it loses moisture at a high rate. Though grass will stand a prolonged period of drought, and will green up again, even when it seemed brown and dead, for best results, water should be applied artificially during dry spells. Of course, in a prolonged drought, it is often the case that the local authority will ban the use of hosepipes. Then, I'm afraid, the lawn must just suffer.

As with any other plant, it is a great mistake in a dry spell, to give the lawn a light sprinkling of water. If you are going to do it at all, give it a thorough soaking. If you just sprinkle a little on the surface, the roots are forced upwards in search of the water, and they will suffer even more when the soil dries out again. The water must be got down to the lower levels, and this means applying a lot.

Obviously, for the busy gardener, a lawn sprinkler is essential. There are all sorts and conditions of automatic machines about, even one that will actually walk itself round the garden automatically. Very nice for the gardener who has lots of lawn and even more money. But, for the smaller garden, I favour those very cheap, small devices, that are no more than a hollow pot with a hole in it. They are stuck in the ground and the water swirls round inside and is then scattered in a fine spray by centrifugal force. The great beauty of them, apart from the price, is that there is absolutely nothing to go wrong. I've had one for years that I bought in Woolies for about 2/9d, and it's still going strong.

For the larger lawn, an oscillating sprinkler is ideal, but you should check first that your water pressure is sufficient to work it well. Don't forget that many local authorities insist that you buy a license for a hosepipe and sprinkler, so you should check that before buying.

Weedkilling

The best way to combat lawn weeds is to avoid them. If you keep the grass growing strongly, it will generally compete successfully. If they do begin to take over, however, they must be removed before they cause large bare patches. I know that some gardeners quite like daisies and dandelions in the lawn to add a bit of colour. Me, I save the wild-flowers for my patch of rough grass, and keep my fine lawn weed-free.

If you only have a few weeds, there is no need to treat the whole lawn. When I go round for my evening 'constitutional', I keep an eagle eye open for weeds. When I see one, I simply cut it out below the surface, with a knife. But, with the deep-rooted perennials, this is not really enough. They'll be back.

With these, it is more effective to use one of the 'spot' weed-killers. Some come in an aerosol can, and others impregnated into a wax stick. Both are very effective.

Larger areas must be treated with an over-all weedkiller. Either use a fertiliser with weedkiller added, or a special herbicide. There are several available both for broad-leaved weeds and for clover. I use one that combines the two.

Again, it is important to apply herbicides at the manufacturer's recommended rate, or damage may occur. If you are using a liquid weedkiller, it is much better to use a sprayer rather than a watering can. Most lawn weedkillers are absorbed through the leaves of the weeds, and transported down to the roots. So, it is most effective if small droplets hang onto the leaves. Once the liquid starts to run off, as it does with a watering-can, very little remains on the leaves to be absorbed. It is also considerably cheaper to use a sprayer, because, of course, less spray is used. If you must use a can, it is worthwhile dividing the lawn up with string lines to ensure an even distribution.

Mulching

Once the lawn is laid, it is obviously impossible to get organic matter underneath the grass by cultivating. You must rely on worms and weather to do that for you.

I mulch my lawn with fine lawn peat, in the autumn. Obviously, it must be done after the last cut, or it simply gets picked up again by the mower. I spread about 1 in. (2.5 cm.) of peat over the grass, and simply allow the rain and the worms to take it down. It obviously works, because there is very little left on the surface by the spring.

As I mentioned before, I also allow the cuttings to go back to the soil on the sandier area of lawn.

Spiking

If the lawn becomes compacted by constant use, water will not penetrate the surface, and the soil will become airless. The best

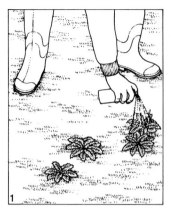

1 Isolated weeds can be killed with a spot weed killer in an aerosol or wax stick

2 Forking will assist aeration and drainage and allow organic matter to work in

3 Raking out the dead grass makes the lawn look greener and allows young grass to 'breathe'

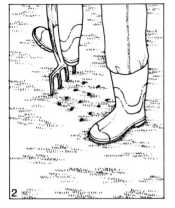

way to relieve compaction is with a hollow-tine fork. This is a special device with hollow, instead of solid spikes. When driven into the soil and pulled out again, it removes a core of soil. This is either removed and replaced with peat in extreme cases, or, more generally, brushed back into the holes.

The holes should be made at about 6 in. (15 cm.) intervals, so you can see that it's a pretty laborious job. It is possible to hire special machines for the job, and well worth the money in my opinion.

A slightly less drastic measure, is to fork the lawn with an ordinary garden fork. This does a lot for aeration, and I do it every year just before I apply the peat mulch. Again, spike at about 6 in. (15 cm.) intervals to the full depth of the fork.

Raking

Every year, a certain amount of grass dies and shrivels up to remain at the base of the plant, at ground level. This 'thatch' must be removed every year, or it will choke the grass and prevent water and nutrients entering the soil. The ideal time for this job is in the spring. I like to leave it there during the winter as an extra protection for the young grass.

Raking out by hand with a spring-tine rake is not the most pleasant job in the world – it does wonders for the stomach muscles, but I can think of better ways to maintain the waistline. However, it must be done. The best thing, I think, is to do it in several bites of no more than fifteen minutes each, or to buy a machine. I must confess that I have succumbed to the temptation, and I'm very glad I did. They run off electricity, and are not over-expensive. Best of all, the rapidly revolving wire combs take out more dead grass in a couple of seconds than I could do in an hour.

Worms

Finally, just a word about our old friend the earthworm. Unless controlled, worms can do a deal of damage to a lawn. The trouble is, they throw up wormcasts, especially in wet weather. The mower runs over these little heaps of fine soil, and flattens them, to form an ideal seed-bed for weeds.

There are plenty of wormkillers available that will polish them off but I don't like the idea. Those worms will also do the lawn a great deal of good, by aerating it for you, and by pulling down into the soil a large quantity of organic matter.

Since the only harm they do is to throw up wormcasts, a much better answer is simply to scatter the heaps before mowing. It is but the work of a moment to quickly run over the lawn with a yard-broom or a besom before using the mower.

THE MIXED BORDER

In common with most modern gardens, the cottage garden at Barnsdale is by no means large and this reduction in the size of today's gardens means that we have to rethink the design concepts. Much of our gardening lore is based on the huge gardens of the latter-day stately homes, where sweeping lawns were flanked by huge borders devoted separately to shrubs, or herbaceous plants, annuals or conifers. Such was the abundance of space, that there were even whole borders devoted to one plant species or one colour. But those days are gone. We no longer have either the space or the time to devote to gardening on this sort of scale.

Even the 'small' cottage gardens of the past were several times larger than the tiny plots allocated to modern estate houses. So, though the principle of mixed planting, which characterised the old cottage gardens, still holds good, it needs some modification to fit the scale of modern gardens.

The principle of cottage garden planting still holds good today, even in modern gardens

In the early stages, annuals will dominate the borders

In the first season at Barnsdale, colour was provided by annuals and a few herbaceous perennials

Planning

While I firmly believe that the garden scheme as a whole should be carefully planned from the start, planting ideas should remain flexible. I know that, even after twenty-five years of gardening, I still often come across new plants or varieties that I want to grow in my garden. That's really a large part of the fun and excitement of gardening. I would much rather build up my borders that way, than to design and plant the borders all in one go, and then never change them.

Mixed borders are, of course, exactly what they say they are. I grow a grand variety of shrubs, hardy herbaceous plants, roses, annuals, biennials, bulbs, herbs, and even decorative vegetables

Even tiny gardens can be crammed with colour

in my borders and there is tremendous scope for imaginative planting. I am also not above moving things round if I feel I have made a mistake, or that I could improve the overall look of the border. There are some plants that resent that sort of treatment and it is these that you must try to get right first time.

The way to go about it, in my opinion, is to start by planting the shrubs. Unlike most of the other 'residents' of the borders, they need several years before they are to be seen at their best. The less disturbance they have, the better and faster they will grow. So, my strategy was to plant the trees and shrubs first, and to adjust the planting of the less permanent subjects around them.

While I agree that, as a general rule, tall plants should be planted at the back of the borders, and short ones at the front, one should not be too rigid about it. The essence of a true mixed border is variety, and this should apply to heights as well as colour and habit. A group of column-shaped conifers, for example, rising from a drift of low planting, adds a great deal of interesting variation.

Correct planting distances, on the other hand, should be strictly adhered to. Many shrubs are only to be seen at their best when they have plenty of room to grow and develop their natural shape. If they are crowded, they tend to become bare on one side, and will always look lop-sided and awkward. This is particularly true of trees. So, find out about your plants first, and plant them wide enough apart to give them room to grow to their natural size. This often seems quite excessive when you are planting small, young material, but those vast expanses of bare soil can always be filled temporarily with annuals and biennials.

Of course, not all plants depend upon their natural shape for their contribution to the border. Many, like roses or most annuals, are there for the colour and shape of their flowers and foliage. These are often best planted in groups to maximise the effect of their massed colour. As the old song tells us, one petunia tends to look a little lonely all on its own. But put it in a drift with a couple of dozen brothers, and the overall effect is different again.

Matching colours is, in my view, something essentially personal. I have often been advised through newspapers or magazines, that to paint the walls of my living room purple and then hang green curtains is definitely not the thing. I am told that my habit of wearing yellow socks with a blue suit is simply not on. Well, if I like purple and green, or blue and yellow, I'll jolly well do it. The same goes for gardens.

I generally tend to go for contrasts. I have planted, for example, a yellow and green variegated *Eleagnus pungens 'Maculata'* just in front of a purple leaved *Cotinus coggyria 'Royal Purple'*. The wine red of the *Cotinus* contrasts completely with the brightly splashed yellow *Eleagnus* and really seems to bring it alive.

Many gardeners though, dislike that sort of stark contrast and prefer more subtle combinations, so it must, in the end, boil down to personal preference.

Foliage patterns should also be taken into consideration. There is a superb border at Powis Castle in Wales, which we visited on *Gardeners' World* some little while ago, where foliage plants have been positioned imaginatively to contrast with each other to form a living tapestry of textures. The effect is quite superb, and has inspired me to careful thought about the positioning of those foliage plants I grow.

I have, for example positioned an ornamental grass *Stipa*

Fatsia japonica

gigantea, near to a *Fatsia japonica* with broad, almost tropical looking leaves, which contrast well with the spiky foliage of the *Stipa*.

So, there is a lot to think about – height, spread, habit, colour and foliage shape. With that number of variables, getting it right first time is almost impossible. But, if you build up the basic bones of the border first, by planting the major shrubs and the trees, you'll have lots of time to think about each separate new plant you buy as you buy it, and you'll be surprised how few mistakes you'll make.

This 'as-you-go-along' planting has another major advantage, which for me was the most important factor. It helps to spread the cost of the final border over as long a period as is necessary. In the meantime, the bare spaces are filled with annuals and biennials which are cheaply raised from seed.

Preparation

Mixed borders are more or less permanent. There will always be the odd spaces where you intend to plant annuals, but in the main, you will only have one opportunity for deep cultivations – before you plant. Once the shrubs start to spread their roots, only the shallowest digging or hoeing should be practised.

At Barnsdale, there is a rock-hard layer of ironstone about a foot below the surface, so I decided to do the job properly and double-dig. This hard pan below the surface is quite a common occurrence in most new gardens. If they have been built on agricultural land, there is likely to be a 'plough-pan' about 9 in. (23 cm.) below the surface. This is generally at the greatest depth of the plough and, after regular annual ploughing, it tends to consolidate and form an almost impenetrable layer.

Modern houses also face another hazard. These days, builders use enormous mechanical diggers to excavate for the foundations of the house. They work in all weathers, compacting the soil to a concrete consistency. They then, almost with malice aforethought, spread the subsoil from the excavations over the concrete pan. That is the way, alas, many a new gardener takes over his first plot. Six inches of subsoil on top of a sheet of concrete. There is often good topsoil beneath, but to get at it, he has to break through with pick and shovel. Not a pretty thought, but certainly a fact of life. I'm afraid I can't even be very encouraging either. It *is* hard work, and there is no other way, but to break through the pan, and try to bring the surface soil into a reasonable state of fertility.

If you have just laid a lawn, either turf or seed, it is unwise to cultivate the border right to the edge of the grass. This will often lead to sinkage until the grass has rooted through well and got a hold. If you must start straight away, as I did, leave about a foot or so of soil near the edge uncultivated and do that later, when the grass is more solid.

Borders can simply be single-dug, but I much prefer to go the whole hog. I'm not too keen on digging holes for plants in hard, uncultivated soil. It is sometimes recommended that, when planting shrubs, you should dig a deep hole, break up the bottom, and then plant. In my experience, unless the surrounding soil is also deeply cultivated, the planting hole tends to act like a drain for all the water for several yards around. In heavy soils especially, this could lead to the hole filling up with water and the roots becoming waterlogged. So, I think it's much better to expend the extra effort and double-dig the lot.

While digging, I worked in a really generous quantity of well rotted manure. If that's difficult, use compost, spent mushroom manure, peat or bark. Apart from working the manure into the bottom spit, I also like to mix a bit into the upper levels as well. This is where the roots will be initially, and it will help give the young plants a good start in life.

If you did the initial weed-killing job properly, there should be no need for weeding. But, if you find roots of perennial weeds while digging, it is as well to remove them. There is no need to apply any fertiliser at this stage. That can go on later, when planting, but it is as well to take a soil test for pH. This will tell you whether your soil is acid or alkaline, and will have a strong bearing on the type of shrubs you eventually choose.

There is, in my opinion, little point in trying to struggle against the natural preferences of plants. Certainly it is possible to grow acid-loving plants like rhododendrons and azaleas in chalky soil. You *can* dig enormous holes, line them with polythene and fill them with peat. But, even after gallons and gallons of Sequestrine, they still never really look happy. It's much better to grow the sort of plants that will thrive in your soil.

At Barnsdale, the pH is 6.5, which is just about ideal, in my opinion. That means that I can grow acid-lovers, while plants that like a slightly more alkaline soil can be coddled with a handful of lime from time to time. As a general rule, I would say that if the pH is above 7.0, you are well advised to stick to plants that will do well in chalky soils. There are plenty of them, so the choice is still very wide. Even with a slightly acid soil, I still plant acid-loving plants in plenty of peat, and I mulch annually just to be on the safe side.

After double digging, the soil is bound to settle a bit and it's advisable to leave it for a few weeks. Even then, the rotting of the organic matter will continue, so the soil will be sinking for some time. It's a good idea, therefore, to keep an eye on new plantings, just to make sure that the roots are always well covered and firmly anchored.

Planting shrubs and roses
Most plants these days, can be bought in containers. There are several advantages with buying this way, but one or two disadvantages too.

Perhaps the most important plus in favour of container-grown plants, is that they can be planted at any time of the year, except when soil conditions prevent it. Shrubs and roses lifted straight from the ground and planted 'bare-rooted' must go in during the dormant season if they are deciduous, and preferably in autumn or spring, if they are evergreen. At that time of year, many plants are without leaves and most won't have flowers, so you need to know what you're buying. Container-grown plants, on the other hand, can be planted in full flower without harm, so you'll have a much better idea of the effect of the plants in relation to their neighbours. Having said that, it is still a much better idea to get to know your plants first in any case. A small plant in a container will give you no notion of its eventual shape and habit. You'll get a much better idea of what the mature plants look like if you see them growing in an established border. There is no substitute for visiting a few of the very good gardens that are open to the public throughout the year and seeing for yourself. Take a notebook with you and you'll come back brimming with ideas.

Bare-rooted plants, are generally cheaper than those sold in containers, and they are very often better quality too. This is more marked in the more vigorous shrubs, and with trees in particular. In an attempt to reduce the high cost of handling container grown plants, they normally have been grown in a pot throughout their lives. With more vigorous shrubs, the root restriction imposed upon them does seem to restrict growth to some degree. I hesitate to say it, but some plants in containers are not kept as well as they could be, once they leave the nursery and get to the garden centre.

If you see plants that look a bit sorry for themselves, with few leaves and roots hanging out of the bottom of the pots, they are best left alone. Of course, I don't intend a general condemnation of container-grown plants or of garden centres. I buy a lot of plants in containers myself, and have generally been satisfied with the quality . But you may need to shop around a bit.

The ability to buy and plant shrubs at any time of the year, has introduced me to one very pleasant aspect of plant collecting. In the course of my job, I visit many fine gardens, nurseries and garden centres all over the country. When I do, I make a point of coming away with a plant. When I plant it, I write on the label when, and where I bought it. A much better memento of happy times than those dreaded holiday snapshots.

It is impossible to give hard and fast rules for planning a planting scheme. So much depends upon the particular size, shape and location of the garden, and so much on personal preference. There may be ugly features that can be hidden with large shrubs, or there may be good views that need to be retained, where tall plantings would be counter-productive.

As I have already suggested, I think the best way a new gardener can tackle this most important aspect of his garden, is to take his time, and fill the borders slowly. The spaces between permanent plantings can always be filled with annuals. But, I do think it's sensible to draw a plan and to work out a scheme for the larger permanent plants at least. Drawing things out on paper certainly does give you a better idea of how the scheme will look eventually, and it also has another great advantage.

Labels tend to get lost, or to fade into illegibility after a few years weathering. If the shrubs are named on a plan, they can easily be relabelled, even if you have forgotten the name.

At Barnsdale, I have one peculiar problem that I am very thankful to have. The garden sits on the top of a hill, with breathtaking views nearly all round. Those views had to be retained. But, at the same time, winds, often of tornado force, tear across the garden from every conceivable direction.

I have tried to plant judiciously, so that tall shrubs shield the garden from the wind, but spaces in between them still allow glimpses of the views. When the shrubs are fully grown, they may well need a little cutting back from time to time, to prevent them obscuring the surrounding countryside altogether. I decided on a mixture of *Berberis* and *Cotoneaster* varieties for my wind-break planting. They are tough, evergreen, tall growing and attractive.

These essential plantings were drawn on the plan first, bearing in mind their eventual spread, to make sure I got the planting distances right.

Planting from containers

The very first job, before planting, is to give all the containers a really good drink. When plants are removed from pots, the young roots tend to stick to the sides, and become damaged. A good soaking will help prevent this. Also, it has been found that a well wetted root ball, helps the plant get over the initial planting shock, even if the soil is dry. But a dry root-ball, even in wet soil, will delay establishment.

Allow the water to drain through the pots, and then set the plants out, still potted, in their final planting positions.

Since the soil has already been well prepared, there is generally no need for extra organic matter. The only exception to this rule is when the soil is very heavy. Then, it is a good idea to put a little peat in the planting hole, and to mix a little more with the soil you replace round the root ball.

Fertiliser will be necessary in all cases. A good rose fertiliser is ideal, though for winter planting, I prefer bonemeal, which consists mainly of phosphates to aid rapid root development. Normally, a good handful scattered onto the soil you have dug out, is adequate.

When you have dug the hole, put the spade across it to give an idea of the required planting height. The top of the root ball should be no more than about 1 in. (2.5 cm.) below the soil surface. Remove the container, set the plant in the hole and refill halfway. Then firm the soil round the root-ball, without actually treading on the roots, fill to the top and firm again. It is very important to ensure that you make a good job of consolidating the soil around the roots, especially if the plants are large. Until

1 Give the containers a good watering and then carefully cut away the container

2 Set the plant at the correct level and firm the soil as the hole is refilled

they root through, they have very little anchorage, and rocking in high winds will damage young roots and delay establishment.

After planting, level the ground around the plants and take out the footmarks with a fork.

In order to prevent surface evaporation of water, spread a good layer of organic matter around the root area and make sure that the soil never becomes dry, until the shrubs have rooted into the soil and can fend for themselves.

On windy sites, it may be necessary to protect shrubs. Evergreens particularly, suffer from rapid water loss in high winds, causing wilting and, in severe cases, browning of the leaves or even complete loss. A temporary screen of hessian or a proprietary plastic windbreak material will go a long way towards solving the problem.

Planting bare-rooted shrubs

Shrubs lifted straight from the field are treated in rather a different way. They must be planted during the dormant season, between November and March if they are deciduous, and in September/October or April/May if they are evergreen.

Sometimes, the more fibrous rooted subjects will be delivered with a hessian or plastic wrapping around the root ball. This should be removed before planting and the root ball should not be disturbed. Otherwise, the planting technique is the same for all bare-rooted plants.

The first golden rule is that the roots must be protected from drying out at all times.

If the plants arrive at a time when there is frost in the ground, they are best left in their parcels in a frost-free shed or garage. If the ground is not frozen but you are not ready to plant, it is better to 'heel' them in. This simply means cutting a trench in a corner of the plot, separating the plants and laying them in the trench. The roots should then be covered with soil and firmed

3 As soon as plants arrive, 'heel' them in. Start by cutting a slit-trench

4 Lay the roots in the trench with the shoots resting on the soil you have dug out

5 Cover the roots with the soil dug out of the next trench

6 Firm the soil round the roots. The plants can then be left until planting time

7 Set bare-rooted plants at the level at which they grew in the nursery

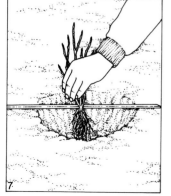

in. They can stay like this for several weeks before planting.

When you are planting, even though the roots will only be exposed for a short time, they should always be kept covered with a piece of sacking or similar material, to prevent wind and sun from drying them out.

If plants arrive with roots that look dry, soak them well by standing them in a bucket of water for three or four hours.

Instead of setting the plants out in their places, I like to stick a cane in at the appropriate spot. Then the lifted plants can stay in one pile with their roots covered.

Dig a hole large enough to take the full spread of the roots. Before setting the plant in the hole, check the roots for damage. Any broken roots should be trimmed back cleanly with a pair of secateurs.

Most plants should be set at the same level they grew to at the nursery or perhaps an inch or so lower. You'll be able to see the soil mark on the stem. There are a few exceptions: plants like roses, flowering currant etc., which grow from a 'stool' sending up new shoots from below ground level, should be planted a few inches deeper.

Cover the roots with fine topsoil, or if the soil is heavy, a mixture of soil and peat. Again, scatter a handful of fertiliser on the heap before refilling. Before completely filling the hole, put a little soil over the roots and shake the plant up and down a bit to ensure that the soil works down between the roots. Then half-fill the hole and firm the soil well with your heel. Firm again after completely refilling.

Planting herbaceous perennials

Most herbaceous plants look best when planted in groups rather than individually. I generally plant in groups of either three or five plants.

Again, you will need to think carefully before positioning the plants, bearing in mind heights, colours, flowering times and foliage texture. Remember that most herbaceous plants die right back to the ground in winter.

If you are planting immediately after the initial preparation of the border, no more cultivation is needed. If the soil has settled down, I like to fork it over before planting and at the same time dig in a general fertiliser.

Herbaceous plants can also be bought in containers, and these can be planted at any time of the year when soil conditions permit. If you buy them bare-rooted, or can pinch a root from a friend's garden, the best times are in September or April.

As with shrubs, pots should be watered well before removing, and bare roots should be kept covered and moist at all times.

Plant with a trowel, setting the roots so that the 'crown' of the plant, where the leaves meet the roots, is at soil level. Firm in with your fingers or with the handle of the trowel, and water well if the soil is dry.

The young shoots of many herbaceous plants are the gourmet slug's favourite food, so it's a wise precaution to sprinkle some slug pellets around new plantings. I like to put those in small heaps and just cover them with a tile or a piece of broken flower-pot. Alas, birds and animals also find slug pellets tasty and a good meal of them will do no good at all.

Herbaceous plants are generally very much cheaper than shrubs, so if the budget is a bit tight, and you're impatient to fill the borders, it's a good plan to plant with herbaceous plants and collect the shrubs slowly as you go along.

As the shrubs grow, the herbaceous plants can be removed to give them room. The great danger is that, because it takes a bit of nerve to dig up an old friend and throw him away, the job is put off, the border becomes overcrowded and the shape of the shrubs is lost.

In the second year, shrubs and herbaceous plants are beginning to spread, but annuals still dominate the Barnsdale borders

Annuals and biennials

The cheapest way to fill the borders with masses of colour while you are waiting for shrubs and herbaceous plants to fill out, is to sow and plant annuals and biennials. In any mixed border, space should be left for them anyway, because there is no better source of colour. By using early spring-flowering biennials, like wall-flowers and forget-me-nots, followed by hardy and half-hardy annuals like petunias, salvias, lobelia and antirrhinums, the borders can be full of colour from early spring until the first frosts.

87

They do have the disadvantage that they have a high labour requirement. In the first year at Barnsdale, when the shrubs were still very small, and the herbaceous plants had not had time to spread, I spent a solid week doing nothing but planting annuals. But they made a terrific show for the whole summer.

The cheapest and easiest of the annuals are the hardy varieties. These can be sown direct in the soil outside, without the protection of glass.

They can be sown at any time between March and late May, but obviously, the earlier the better. There is, however, no point in sowing until the soil has started to warm up a little after the winter frosts. If it is cold and wet, the seed will lie in the ground for a long time before germinating, and there is then the risk of rotting. Optimum sowing time will depend upon location and soil type. Here in the Midlands and on light, sandy soil that warms up quickly, I like to sow hardy annuals during early April. In some years, of course, this has to be delayed if spring starts cold and wet. In the south of the country, I would suggest that sowing could take place from the middle of March, while in the far north it is best left until early May.

I fork the ground over before sowing, working in a dressing of Growmore at about 4 oz per sq.yd (120 gm per sq.m.).

Annuals and biennials should always be planted or sown in drifts, rather than individually or in straight rows. They make a much more effective mass display of colour that way. There are one or two exceptions, where tall-growing plants are used as 'spot' plants to add height to a drift of low planting, but generally, the massed effect is much to be preferred.

So, after digging and raking to a fine tilth, mark out the position of the drifts by scratching a line in the soil.

Then, in each marked out area, I sow in shallow drills, about 6 in. (15 cm.) apart. The seed *can* be scattered over the whole area and raked in or covered with sieved soil, but I prefer the drill method. When the young seedlings germinate, it is much easier to keep the weeds down if they are in rows. Not only are the seedlings easily distinguishable from weed seedlings because there are several of the same type in a straight line, but it is also possible to get a hoe between the rows.

When the young plants are large enough to handle, they can be thinned out to about 6 in. (15 cm.) apart, and the thinnings can, if desired, be transplanted into another part of the border.

After that all you need to do is to water if the soil is dry, and stake taller plants with a few twiggy pea sticks.

Half-hardy annuals need to be raised in a greenhouse or conservatory, and are therefore a much more expensive proposition. They do, however, increase the range considerably. They can be bought as bedding plants, but they are, alas, getting very expensive these days.

Sowing starts in late January or early February with things like lobelia and geraniums. They are generally sown in boxes or pots of compost and transferred at a wider spacing, to seed trays when they are large enough to handle.

It is essential to get these tender plants gradually used to the cooler temperatures outside. If you plant straight from the warmth of the greenhouse, they will harden up and stop growing. It takes some time before they trust you enough to get going again afterwards. So a cold-frame is essential. They should be put into it sometime during late April or early May, and the lights should be left closed for a day or two. Gradually, they are opened wider during the day, and shut down again at night. When they are removed altogether during the day, a little ventilation is put on at night, gradually increasing, until the lights are removed altogether round about the last week in May.

They should be planted out no earlier than the last week in May in the south and the first or even second week in June in the north.

If you buy plants from a nursery, you must make sure that they too have been properly hardened off. Never buy bedding plants straight from a greenhouse unless you intend to harden them off yourself at home.

Planting is much the same as for sowing hardy annuals. Again, dig over the ground, apply fertiliser and plant in drifts. I generally plant with my fingers, but if your soil is stony or there is a chance of tiny pieces of glass in it, then it is safer, though more long-winded, to use a trowel. After planting make sure that the young plants do not go dry.

Bulbs, corms and tubers

Perhaps the easiest way to fill the borders with colour is with bulbs, corms and tubers. Many of them can be left in the ground, where they will come up year after year, unfailingly producing a wealth of bloom. Somehow, spring just wouldn't be spring without that welcome splash of colour after the drearier winter months.

The flowering year at Barnsdale starts with shy little snowdrops hanging their heads at the sight of their brasher, more colourful cousins, the crocuses. And from then on, there is always something in flower. They are followed by delightful small botanical tulips, and narcissi of almost every shade of yellow, pink, white and orange. Set against the cheerful blue of the chionodoxas and scillas, they are a sure sign that spring is really here.

By mid-April, it's the turn of the tulips, and they flower right through until the end of May. In the summer, there are gladioli, lilies, montbretia and freesias, and, of course, those most floriferous of flowering plants, the dahlias.

I use bulbs dotted throughout the borders, some of which I leave in all the time, and others I lift and store for the winter, to be planted again the following year. They may not be cheap initially, but they certainly give value for money over the years.

Bulbs make a bright display in the spring

In the cottage garden, formal bedding schemes are out. I hate to see lines of tulips and hyacynths standing to attention like soldiers. That may be all right in the park, but it looks out of place in the more informal setting of the cottage garden. With the possible exception of the tall, striking subjects like lilies or canna, they should not be planted singly either. Bulbs make a much more arresting display if they are set out in drifts. They are particularly good for providing colour in places that would

Informal planting of bulbs look more 'at home' in the cottage garden

otherwise be dull. For example, I have planted several spring-flowering bulbs in between the roses. The smaller crocuses, botanical tulips and miniature narcissi brighten up that part of the border when the roses are contributing nothing but bare stems. Of course, you have to be careful not to provide too much competition. Taller daffodils and narcissi, for example, would choke the rose bushes with foliage until June or July.

Spring bulb planting starts in August, with the daffodils and narcissi. Dig over the soil, forking in a dressing of bonemeal at 2oz per sq.yd (60gm per sq.m.), and plant the bulbs with a trowel. On average, they should be covered with about 4in. (10cm.) of soil, though the smaller bulbs need not go so deep. It is better to err on the deep side if anything. If they are planted too shallow, there is a tendency to produce 'blind' flower stems.

The remainder of the spring-flowering bulbs can be planted from September onwards. Though it is possible to go on planting until November, it is preferable to get the job done as soon as possible after the end of August.

Summer-flowering bulbs are generally planted from March onwards, depending upon the site and the locality. Tender plants like dahlias should not be planted too early. They are very susceptible to frost damage, so the trick is to plant the tubers at a time when the first emerging young shoots will be safe from the danger of frost. Generally, if they are planted in April, they will be safe. These tender plants cannot be left in the ground over winter or the tubers will succumb to the wet and cold. As soon as the first frost touches the leaves, they should be lifted, dried out and stored in a frost-free shed.

Autumn-flowering bulbs like colchicum and hardy cyclamen, have a charm all their own. They are generally not as striking in colour as their spring-flowering cousins, but their soft, pastel shades go well with the autumn foliage colour. They should be planted during July and August.

Climbers

The last thing anyone could say about me is that I'm house-proud. I must confess that I spend too much time outside in the garden to worry about what the inside looks like. So, my house is not so much somewhere to live, as something to grow things up! Again, Fortune has favoured me and given me two fairly warm walls – one facing south-west and the other south-east. This means that I'm able to grow a few of the more exotic climbing plants as well as the hardier types on the two colder, shaded walls.

There is a popular misconception that climbing plants damage the walls by pulling out the mortar, or making them damp. Frankly, they have never caused me any trouble at all. The only time I have seen any damage, is when strong-growing wild ivy has been pulled from the side of a house, when a bit of mortar did come with it. I have never seen any problems with the cultivated self-clinging climbers, and certainly, those that need to be trained on wires or trellis are completely trouble-free.

I have found wooden trellis an expensive way of supporting climbers, and I don't like the look of plastic netting. I support all those climbers that need it, by fixing wires to wooden lathes screwed to the walls. They look unobtrusive, and are much cheaper.

When planting climbers, provision must be made for the fact that the soil next to walls is likely to be much drier than the rest of the border. Very often, the rain will not reach right up to the wall, because the overhanging eaves prevent it. Also the warmth from the wall will help dry out the soil faster. So make sure that there is plenty of organic matter in the soil, and plant about 1 ft (30 cm.) away from the wall. Even then, it is worth checking the soil from time to time, and watering by hand if necessary. Once the plants have rooted, they will search for water further out in the border.

Climbing roses make a fine show of colour in the summer,

but it should be borne in mind that they contribute little in winter and early spring. In fact, when I first came to Barnsdale, one of the only two cultivated plants in the garden was a climbing *'Ena Harkness'*. It was a very old specimen though, and I wasn't too keen on the deep red colour, which tended to merge with the red of the brickwork. So, I hardened my heart, pulled it out and replaced it with a yellow *'Golden Showers'*. This one has a very long flowering period, and makes a bright show against the red brick.

There are plenty of climbing roses to choose from and varieties that can be grown against walls facing any direction. When training them, it's a good idea to tie the shoots low down, almost horizontally, since this will increase flowering.

Perhaps the most popular of all climbers, are the *Clematis* varieties. I particularly like the small-flowered species, and I have used *C. montana rubens* to cover an ugly drainpipe on the south-west facing wall. On the same wall, the front door seemed to me to cry out for that most traditional of clematis, *C. jackmanii 'Superba'*. The giant purple flowers are a common site in many gardens, but not, in my view to be missed. Clematis, while liking a sunny spot, need a cool, moist root-run, so the area round the roots is best shaded. Mine will spread its roots under the paving near the front door, but I have also spread a thick layer of gravel on the soil round the roots.

Above: *Clematis jackmanii 'Superba'*
Right: *Clematis montana rubens*

Contrasting with the bronze foliage of the species clematis, I have planted the grey leaved *Teucrium fruticans*. This is really a wall shrub rather than a climber, and needs tying in regularly. If you have a warm wall, this one really gives value for money. The silvery foliage is evergreen, and is spotted with small blue flowers most of the summer.

On the south-east wall, I have planted another wall shrub – *Abutilon megapotanicum* 'Kentish Belle'. All summer long, this one is a mass of delightful orange/yellow lanterns.

North, or north-east walls are considered a problem, but there are, in fact, many quite showy climbers that will thrive in the colder conditions. I have used three hardy, but nonetheless highly attractive climbers. *Parthenocissus henryana* is a decidedly superior Virginia Creeper. The green leaves are delicately veined with white, and the red autumn colour is a sight to behold.

Next to that, hiding another drainpipe, is an ivy, *Hedera helix* 'Goldheart'. The green leaves of this relative of the common ivy, are splashed with a brilliant golden centre. Both these are self-clinging, so they need no support.

Pyracantha 'Mojave' may need a little support in the early stages, but it will soon grow stiff and straight, close to the wall. I just hold the odd branch with a lead-headed wall nail. Another evergreen, the bright white spring flowers are followed in the autumn with brilliant orange berries.

Abutilon megapotanicum
'Kentish Belle'

Right: *Parthenocissus henryana*
Below right: *Pyracantha* 'Mojave'

THE SHADE BORDER

Most gardens have some areas that are in full or partial shade, and Barnsdale is no exception. But, far from looking upon this as a disadvantage or a problem, I consider it a great asset. It provides a superb opportunity for making a cool, green part of the garden, in contrast to the bright, colourful borders in the sun.

There is a great variety of plants that will either do well in shady places, or actually require shade to some degree. Obviously the same soil considerations apply, particularly as far as acidity is concerned. Though acid lovers, like rhododendrons, will thrive in dappled shade, it would not be sensible to plant them in chalky soil. It is also important to take into account the reason for the lack of sunlight. If, for example, the planting area is shaded by large trees, the ground is likely to be dry and hungry. There are plants that will do well in such situations, but they are quite different to those that like a shady, moist spot. The amount of shade also has a bearing on choice of plants. Some will do well in the light, dappled shade provided by tree cover, but will not be happy in the dense shade of a north-facing wall.

Of course, most borders in small gardens have a fair mixture of shaded and sunny spots, so there is ample scope for planting all types.

At Barnsdale, there are two 'problem' spots. One is the border on the north side of the house, one end of which gets a little sun in the morning, while the other remains in deep shade all day. The other area is under the shade of trees, bordering my bit of woodland, which is the perfect spot for woodland shade-lovers like ferns.

The first job was to cover the walls with climbers – the Virginia Creeper, ivy and pyracantha I described in the previous chapter. I also took the opportunity of planting a *Camellia 'Donation'*, bought on my travels, from the beautiful garden at Borde Hill, where *'Donation'* was raised. Camellias prefer the shade of a north wall, because the early morning sunlight on frozen blooms in the early spring, will knock them down like ninepins. Given the chance to thaw out slowly, they come to no harm.

In the same border, I was able to indulge myself with a collection of my favourite herbaceous plants – *Hostas*. The 'Plantain Lilies' as they are commonly known, are ideal shade-loving plants, though the green-leaved varieties will do well in sunlight also. As foliage plants they are, in my opinion, unsurpassed, and some have the added bonus of attractive flowers too.

In the part of the border that is only partly shaded, I planted the American varieties *'Honeybells'* which has large, shapely

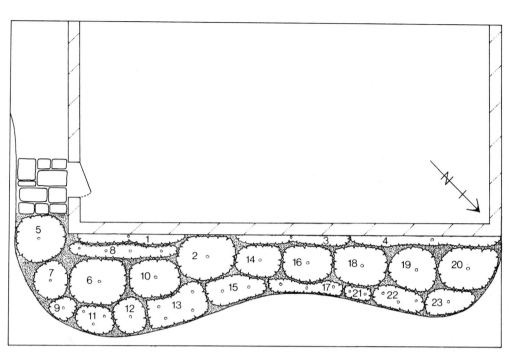

Hosta fortunei 'Aurea'

green leaves and deep purple, scented flowers, and 'Royal Stan-dard' which again sports large green leaves, but this time with white, scented flowers.

The variegated varieties give rise to a lot of head-scratching because all of them are quite outstanding, so it's difficult to choose. One day, I'm determined to have them all. For the time being, I settled for *H. fortunei 'Aurea Marginata'* which has large, green leaves, edged with a margin of gold. The purple flowers

97

in summer are an added bonus. I couldn't resist *H. fortunei* '*Picta*', because, although the cream-edged green leaves tend to turn greener as the season progresses, it is one of the first to show in spring, when you know the others won't be far behind.

Perhaps the most striking of all the variegated Hostas is *H. ventricosa* '*Medio Variegata*'. The deep green leaves are splashed with great patches of striking yellow, while 3 ft (1 m.) spikes of lavender flowers appear in late summer.

My all-time favourite is *H. sieboldiana* '*Elegans*'. There's really only one word to describe this one – regal. It produces enormous leaves of dark blue-green topped by pale lilac spikes of flowers in late summer.

Hostas really need different foliage patterns to set them off, so I have planted other plants with more fern-like foliage around them. In the lightly shaded areas, the finely divided, bronze leaves of *Acer palmatum* '*Atropurpureum*' make an interesting contrast, while in the heavier shade, *Astilbe* '*Bressingham Beauty*' completes the pattern.

All these plants require a moist soil, so I have used plenty of organic matter in the initial preparation, and I top that up with an annual mulch.

It somehow seems odd that such a floriferous plant as *Hydrangea hortensis* should thrive in shady conditions. It makes such a bright show of pinks, white and reds and even blue on acid soil that it looks as though it should be at home in full sun. But, provided there is sufficient moisture, these showy plants will do well in shade.

Above (top): *Hosta fortunei* '*Picta*'

Above: *Hosta ventricosa* '*Medio Variegata*'

Left: *Hydrangea hortensis*

Above: *Hypericum calycinum*

Right: *Astilbe 'Bressingham Beauty'*

Helleborus niger

In dappled shade, the *Hypericums* are invaluable. They range in size from the ground-coverer *H. calycinum* to large, spreading varieties like *H. Hidcote*, that reach 6 ft (2 m.). Most are ever-green or semi-evergreen, and bear a profusion of bright yellow, saucer-shaped flowers. For heavy shade, the dwarfer *H. caly-cinum* and *H. androsaemum* are to be preferred.

Ground coverers are very useful for suppressing weeds and reducing labour, and two that will also do well in shade are the 'Partridge Berry' *Gaultheria procumbens*, which has glossy green leaves and bright red berries, and *Paschysandra terminalis* another evergreen, with prettily shaped leaves and greenish white flowers in early spring.

The bushy habit of the herbaceous Geraniums makes them excellent weed-supressors too, though some of them are by no means dwarf. *G. psilostemon*, for example, will grow to 4 ft (1.2 m.) tall with a stunning show of red flowers in summer, though the deeply-cut foliage is reward enough for me.

Superb both in foliage and in flower are the hellebores. The Christmas Rose, *Helleborus niger* is a welcome sight in the early spring. I must confess that I have never got it to flower at

Left: *Helleborus orientalis*
Below: *Helleborus foetidus*

Above (top): *Primula sieboldii*
'Snowflake'

Above: *Primula denticulata*

Right: *Mahonia aquifolium*

Christmas at Barnsdale. A little later comes the Lenten Rose, *H. orientalis* while the handsome pale-green flowers and divided foliage of *H. foetidus* make it a 'must', especially for flower arrangers.

If you have a partially shaded area with plenty of moisture in the soil, you mustn't miss the delightful primulas. There are several different types, but perhaps the easiest to grow, and certainly the most popular, is *P. 'Wanda'*. A close relation of the primrose, it forms close mats of flower ranging in colour from purple/red, through pink and blue to white. Another short, mat-former is *P. sieboldii*, and the best variety here is *'Geisha Girl'*, a fine pink form.

The 'Drumstick Primulas', *P. denticulata* produce their flowers on tall stems, and the colours range from white, through pink and red to purple.

Really dry shade can be a problem, and the choice here is somewhat more limited. Perhaps the easiest shrub of all, is the accommodating *Mahonia aquifolium*. This will produce bright yellow clusters of flowers but perhaps its greatest asset is the glossy green foliage, which turns a deep bronze/red in winter. Many *Cotoneasters* will do well in difficult, dry areas, and these

are triply useful, bearing white flowers followed by red or orange berries, with many varieties retaining their leaves in winter.

I must admit, that I had not fully realised the tremendous range of hardy ferns available, until I visited a specialist nursery for *Gardeners' World*. After seeing them, I had to build myself a small fern garden.

Most ferns like a shady spot and a fairly moist soil. If it is likely to dry out in the heat of the summer, they will certainly suffer, though there are varieties that, even then, will recover after a shower of rain.

I am lucky to have a corner of my garden heavily shaded by trees, but with moist, peaty soil. It is ideally placed right next to my little copse, so it's an ideal spot for ferns and other woodland plants.

I started by digging it over and working in a very generous dressing of manure. I like to be on the safe side. I then spent a day digging out a couple of old tree-stumps from the woods, and setting these in the centre of the area to be planted. They are there to serve two purposes. Firstly, they are very decorative, with small ferns now peeping out from the base. But they also serve a more practical purpose. The roots of the ferns can run underneath the stumps, where their shade will ensure that the soil is always moist and cool.

Certainly the most common fern to be seen both in the wild and in cultivation is the 'Male Fern' *Dryopteris filix-mas*. This is

Dryopteris filix-mas

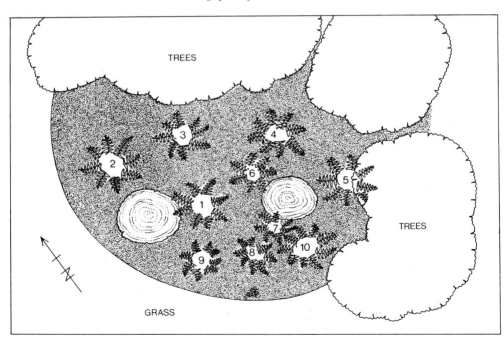

1 Before planting ferns, dig plenty of organic matter into the soil

2 An old tree-stump looks quite attractive and serves to provide a cool root-run

3 Plant with a trowel, setting the plants at the level they grew on the nursery

4 After planting, mulch the whole area with peat or composted bark

5 In the first year in particular, it is essential to make sure the plants are well watered

Fern border
1 *Polypodium vulgare cornubiense*
2 *Dryopteris filix-mas*
3 *Dryopteris pseudo-mas* '*Grandaceps Askew*'
4 *Dryopteris cristata* '*Jackson*'
5 *Dryopteris filix-mas*
6 *Cyrtomium falcatum* '*Rochfordianum*'
7 *Asplenium scolopendrium*
8 *Asplenium trichomanes*
9 *Asplenium scolopendrium* '*Alto*'
10 *Asplenium scolopendrium* '*Treble*'

the one with feathery fronds that is often seen growing wild in woodland. It will grow quite tall, sometimes up to 5 ft (1.5 m.), and has the advantage of being evergreen. There are several different forms of the Male Fern with crisped and crested fronds, all of which are quite easy to grow.

Perhaps one of the most graceful of ferns, is the 'Maidenhair Spleenwort', *Asplenium trichomanes*. This looks very much like the Maidenhair fern sold as a pot-plant. So dainty and delicate are its fronds that it really looks as though it shouldn't be hardy at all. Though they like a moist situation, the Spleenworts detest bad drainage, so they should not be planted where the soil is likely to become waterlogged.

A great favourite of mine is another *Asplenium*, the relatively common *A. scolopendrium*, known as the 'Harts-Tongue Fern'. The fronds are shiny green and strap-shaped with attractively wrinkled edges. Again, it has the advantage of being evergreen.

And, if evergreens appeal, the 'Common Polypody', *Polypodium vulgare* is not to be missed. The smooth, lance-shaped

Above: *Vinca major*
Left: *Polypodium vulgare*
Right: *Pieris forrestii 'Forest Flame'*

fronds are very deeply cut to give it an attractive, comb-like appearance. In common with a few other ferns, it has a creeping rootstock, so it's likely to appear some feet away, once it's established.

After planting all ferns, they deserve special attention, at least for the first year. The main chore is to see that they are well watered. They will take a little while to root deep down in the moister soil, so if dry weather prevails, they will be grateful for a really good soaking from time to time. I simply put the lawn sprinkler on the border for a few hours about once a week. They will also benefit from an annual mulch with peat or ground bark, to add humus and avoid surface evaporation. I like ground bark particularly in this situation because it adds to the woodland look.

At the back of my fern garden, I have planted a few acid-loving shrubs, which also thrive in shaded situations. *Rhododendrons* and *Azaleas* make a striking show of colour in the spring, and the bright red young leaves of *Pieris forrestii 'Forest Flame'*, make a grand show over a long period. I rarely have weed problems under these plants because of the shade and the heavy dressings of ground bark I put on every year. But, just to be sure, I have planted a few roots of *Vinca major*. This Periwinkle is an excellent ground coverer, and it dots the ground with blue flowers from April until the end of June.

Another excellent ground coverer for shady places, is the Winter Aconite, *Eranthis hyemalis*. These tuberous-rooted perennials spread rapidly to form mats of emerald green, topped by bright yellow flowers. And, for something a bit different, I have also planted *Eranthis cilicica* which has much the same appearance except that the leaves are rather more divided and have a bronze tinge.

Bulbs fascinate me and I can rarely resist spending much more than I can afford in the garden centre in late summer. So, when I went in to buy the Aconites, I also came out with several others I had decided to leave until next year.

Hardy cyclamen naturalise extremely well in shady spots under trees or at the foot of a north-facing wall. As the years go by, they increase in size dramatically, and I have seen them with corms as big as dinner plates. Their flowers are very much like those of their half-hardy relatives that are so popular as pot-plants. There are three autumn flowering species which I think are well worth growing. *C. neapolitanum* is perhaps the most popular and deservedly so, the rosy-pink flowers develop just before the leaves, in August/September and make a charming show. The variety *C. n. album* has white flowers and beautifully mottled foliage.

These varieties can be followed in February or March, by *C. coum* which has pinky red flowers. Better still, and flowering at the same time, is *C. ibericum* which has pink or crimson flowers according to variety, and has the added advantage of silver marbled foliage.

Many of the cultivated forms of woodland bulbs are well suited to shady places. The Dogs Tooth Violet (*Erithronium*), Snowdrops (*Galanthus*), Bluebells (*Scilla*) and the Wood Anemone (*A. nemorosa*) all look excellent underneath trees and shrubs, or in shady places in the border.

Eranthis hyemalis

Cyclamen neapolitanum

THE SCENTED BORDER

Plants are not just pretty faces. Though the sight of a colourful border is probably the greatest reward for our gardening efforts, we cannot overlook their second major contribution to the quality of our lives. One of the great pleasures of gardening and gardens, is the unique perfume to be enjoyed from a well stocked border. Even the smell of a freshly cut lawn makes you stop and catch your breath for a moment, taking you back to those well remembered summer days in the country. The delicate perfumes and heady smells of summer are a pleasure not to be missed.

Blind people, of course, appreciate perfume even more, and I have seen many a blind gardener's pleasure from perfume alone. Indeed, it was on a visit to a blind gardener, that I was so struck by the wealth of different fragrances from the border, that I determined to have one of my own. This amazing lady knew the names and colours of every single plant in that garden, and yet she had never seen one of them. All were recognised by their distinctive perfume.

As cultivated plants have been bred and selected for bigger blooms and better colours, fragrance has often been bred out. Alas, some of our best sweet-peas, and most beautiful roses are something of a disappointment when it comes to fragrance. You can't have it all ways, and often, where colour, size and form have been improved, the perfume has been impaired or lost altogether.

But that is not always the case. There are still plenty of annuals, perennials and shrubs to choose from, whose perfume is a delight. When you come home from a hard day at work, clogged up with the modern-day stink of exhaust fumes and fast-food shops, that's just the tonic you need.

I have just the area in my garden at Barnsdale, tailormade for a perfumed garden. I deliberately left a narrow border around my paved 'sun-trap' area so that I could fill it with spring and summer perfume. This is the spot where I sit, whenever the weather is good enough, to relax, eat my meals out in the fresh air, and entertain my friends. Here, the sun is hot and the air is tranquil. What better place for a perfumed garden?

When I planned the border, I was in lyrical mood, and becoming euphoric, all to myself, about the joys of scented plants. When I came to prepare it, my mood changed, and my lyrical language gradually became more colourful until it bordered on the obscene! The reason for this Jekyll and Hyde transformation, was over thirty barrow-loads of rubble that had to be dug out and carted away before I could entrust the soil with my chosen few. But there was no alternative, no short cut. Out it

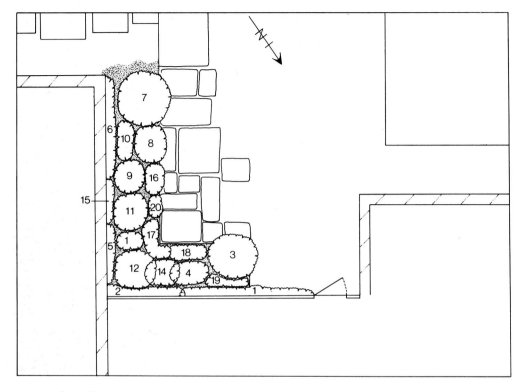

came, to be refilled with a mixture of good garden soil and well-rotted manure. Now it's finished, that border should grow plants better than anywhere else in the garden. Normally, I would have prepared the border in the same way as the others, by double digging and working in plenty of organic matter.

Climbers

The first job was to fix wires to the wall and fence that surround the paved area, preparatory to planting. As before, I simply fixed wooden battens to the wall with rawlplugs and screws, screwed in some galvanised 'eyes' and fixed galvanised wire to them. This is perfectly adequate for climbers and wall shrubs that need to be tied in. But for plants that support themselves by twining, vertical wires are needed also. I used thinner, plastic coated wire, twisted round the horizontal wires, to form a square mesh. The wires are set about 1 ft (30 cm.) apart, both horizontally and vertically.

There are plenty of climbing and rambling roses that are heavily perfumed, and a quick look through a catalogue will soon indicate which have the most powerful scent. I decided that, since I had climbing roses elsewhere, I would settle for shrubs.

Scented borders
1 Lonicera periclymenum
2 Lonicera japonica 'Halliana'
3 Skimmia laureola
4 Daphne mezereum
5 Jasminium officinale
6 Wisteria sinensis
7 Ceanothus 'Gloire de Versailles'
8 Yucca filamentosa
9 Ceanothus thyrsiflorus
10 Philadelphus 'Belle Etoile'
11 Viburnum bodnantense
12 Viburnum juddii
13 Osmarea 'Burkwoodii'
14 Osmanthus delavayi
15 Clematis montana
16 Santolina incana
17 Lavandula angustifolia 'Hidcote'
18 Myrtus communis
19 Convallaria majalis

Lonicera periclymenum 'Belgica'

If you ask anyone, gardener or layman, to name a fragrant climber, he will say 'Honeysuckle'. There can be no better plant for perfume than our native wild honeysuckle *Lonicera periclymenum*. If you're over thirty, you have almost certainly seen this delightful plant scrambling through hedgerows in the country. Now, alas, modern farming methods seem intent on destroying the hedgerows themselves and, of course, the honeysuckle with them. All the more reason why we should perpetuate the species in our gardens.

There are two varieties of common honeysuckle in cultivation. Strangely for a British plant, they both have Dutch names, but are none the worse for that. *L. p. 'Belgica'* is known as the 'Early Dutch Honeysuckle' and flowers during May and June. The profuse blooms are reddish on the outside, fading to yellow. A little later, from July to October comes the reddish/ purple flowered 'Late Dutch Honeysuckle', *L. p. 'Serotina'*.

But, for me, the best perfume comes from the common or garden 'Woodbine', *L. periclymenum*, which is purplish on the outside and creamy white within. Another good one is *L. japonica 'Halliana'*, and that is readily available at most nurseries. The white flowers turn yellow as they get older, are very fragrant and produced over a long period. There are, of course, several other good varieties and species of honeysuckle, but none, in my opinion, to match the perfume of our native Woodbine.

Another fairly common climber, which has been grown in cottage gardens since the sixteenth century, is the 'Common White' Jasmine, *Jasminium officinale*. This is a strong-growing, twining plant that bears a profusion of deliciously scented white flowers from June to September. In the north of the country, it may be wise to select a warm, sheltered wall for this one, though in the south it is perfectly hardy.

I suppose the noblest of all climbing plants is the 'Chinese Wisteria', *W. sinensis*. A strong growing twiner, it will easily cover a high wall, and in May and June, is a sight to be seen. Long, drooping racemes of deep blue flowers appearing before the leaves, make it a rare spectacle indeed. There are other varieties of this superb plant, producing white, lilac and dark purple flowers, but for me, the blue flowered forms are best in colour and fragrance. I must say that I have had some difficulty establishing my wisteria. They do seem to take at least a season to make enough root to get them growing vigorously, so don't be discouraged if they don't get away well in the first year. They will almost certainly make up for it later.

If you need really rampant growth, perhaps for covering an ugly drainpipe, there is no better bet than *Clematis montana*. This popular clematis bears masses of flowers in May, and is happy

Wisteria sinensis

even on a north facing wall. The variety *C. m. 'Alexander'* is particularly good. The flowers are creamy white and highly perfumed.

When it comes to shrubs, perennials and annuals, there is plenty of choice, so I was able to select a few of my true favourites.

I suppose my favourite perfumed plant is *Daphne mezereum*, though I don't believe it to be the most decorative plant in the world. To tell you the truth, it carries with it, for me, nostalgic memories of youthful romance. But that's another story entirely. The purple/red flowers carried in profusion in February and March, though they make a welcome show at a difficult time of the year, are perhaps a little dull. That is, I suppose, a matter of personal taste, but there can be no argument about the perfume. It is absolutely delicious, and very strong indeed. The forms *D. m. 'Grandiflora'* and *'Rosea'* are distinct improvements on the flower size and colour.

To really fill my scented corner with perfume in spring, I planted a *Skimmia laureola*. Again, I suppose that some would say there are better Skimmias for colour, but this one beats them all for perfume. It makes a small, bushy evergreen, bearing a mass of greenish yellow flowers which are very sweetly scented. Unlike most other Skimmias, the male and female flowers are borne on different plants. So, if you want the bright red berries, you'll need a plant of each sex.

Daphne mezereum

I don't do a lot of sitting about outside during the winter, but you never know when you might get a good day when it's possible. So, determined to maintain a succession of flowers, I have planted a *Viburnum bodnantense*. This is a winner in any garden, because it flowers profusely during the winter months, on and off from October onwards. The flowers are a rich pink, beautifully fragrant and amazingly frost-hardy. Well worth a place in any border.

Viburnum bodnantense

Another favourite viburnum is *V. juddii* which flowers later, in April and May. The flowers start as tight buds of pink, and open to white, making a multicoloured flower head. A good shrub for small gardens or restricted borders, in that it remains small and bushy.

I wouldn't like to say that *Ceanothus* was as richly fragrant as some of the others I have mentioned, but I had to grow two plants in my border. They are, for me, the best of the blue flowered shrubs, bar none. *C. 'Gloire de Versailles'* makes a fairly large plant, which is covered in sprays of powder-blue flowers most of the summer and autumn. In complete contrast of form, is *C. thyrsiflorus repens*. This grows into a large mound of evergreen foliage which covers itself in slightly fragrant, Cambridge blue flowers in early summer. This one is pretty hardy though, as with all ceonothus, it's worth giving them a sheltered site. *'Gloire de Versailles'*, in fact, really needs the reflected warmth of a wall to survive in more northerly areas.

Ceanothus thyrsiflorus repens

Osmarea 'Burkwoodii'

A plant that will cause no problems of hardiness, is *Osmarea 'Burkwoodii'*. It makes a compact shrub, ideal for small gardens, and the dark, shiny leaves and pure white flowers in April and May, are a joy. Closely related is *Osmanthus delavayi* which has small, holly-like leaves and bears a profusion of fragrant white flowers in April.

For sheltered spots only, is the 'Mexican Orange Blossom', *Choisya ternata*. Both the dark green leaves and exotic white flowers are sweetly scented, and it will do well in sun or shade.

When I had planted that lot, leaving space for a few scented annuals and herbaceous perennials, I paused for breath. I had already crammed the border fairly full, and was concerned that I might get carried away with enthusiasm. However, I do feel that small areas like this one, should be, if anything, overplanted. An area of paving always tends to look somewhat 'hard', and if it is surrounded by high walls on three sides, it can be a bit claustrophobic too. The answer, is to fill it with plants, to give a really lush, almost tropical effect.

Well, there's one tropical looking plant that is hardy and perfumed, that had to be there. *Yucca filamentosa* is a native of South America, and it really looks the part. Great spiky leaves form a sort of rosette of foliage, and from these rise tall stems of pendu-

Choysia ternata

lous flowers, white and scented. It does need a sunny spot to do well, and good drainage is essential.

Amongst the shrubs, I had left room for annuals and herbaceous perennials. One that no scented border can be without, is lily-of-the-valley, *Convallaria majalis*. The white, bell-shaped and highly perfumed flowers need no description. It does best in partial shade, so I underplanted it amongst the shrubs. I may have to thin it out in future years, because, when it gets overcrowded, it tends to lose vigour.

Late summer is often a tricky time for flowers of any sort, and harder still if fragrance is needed. I filled some of this gap by planting corms of *Acidanthera bicolor murielae*. This produces tall stems, each bearing five or six flowers, white with a large, striking maroon blotch in the centre.

Convallaria majalis

There are several other bulbs that will provide a brilliant show of colour, coupled with a heady perfume. *Hyacinths* are an obvious choice for the spring. They are rather more expensive than other bulbous subjects and should really be lifted from year to year in order to allow them to dry out and rest a little before being planted again. Not so well known, is the 'Summer Flowering Hyacinth', *Galtonia candicans*. This is a much larger plant than the spring-flowering type, producing flower spikes some 4 ft (120 cm.) high. There are generally twenty or more sweetly scented white flowers on each spike, and they can be left in the ground to form quite large clumps.

Lilium auratum

Lilies are also tall plants for the back of the border or they can be used to great effect in clumps of three or more, to give height to a low planting. My favourite for perfume is *Lilium auratum* which has white flowers spotted crimson, with a distinctive yellow stripe on each petal. A regal plant indeed.

Though my scented border has been planted rather more fully than the other borders, there are still bare spaces to allow the permanent plants room to expand. Temporarily at least, these can be filled with annuals. I am particularly fond of those which fill the evening air with perfume. At that time of the day, the persistent wind at Barnsdale tends to take a rest. No doubt reserving its energy for a good blow the next day. On a warm summer evening, I like to take my evening constitutional round the 'estate', generally with my head full of what has to be done the following day. When the wind has gone to bed, these annuals really come into their own, filling the garden with a delicious perfume.

Nicotiana affinis

Flowering tobacco plants are, in my opinion, one of the best of scented flowers. The one to go for is the white-flowered *Nicotiana affinis* which, though perhaps not so flamboyant in colour, as some of the other varieties, certainly beats them all for perfume.

Two others deserve a special mention for their contribution to the scented garden at this time of the day. Night-scented Stock, *Matthiola bicornis* has lilac blossoms, but is generally grown as its common name implies, for its very strong evening perfume. *Mignonette* has red flowers and a superb perfume.

While one must naturally look to flowers to provide maximum perfume, there are some plants whose scent is in their foliage. This is not always immediately apparent, and it is necessary to work a little for your pleasure, by picking a leaf and crushing it in your fingers. I have included a few such plants in my scented border, and the range of such different perfumes is quite surprising.

Lavender is an obvious choice, and will certainly need no introduction. The grey leaves and deep blue flowers are an almost obligatory requirement in the cottage garden. There are several varieties available at nurseries ranging from the dwarf *Lavandula angustifolia 'Nana Alba'*, which actually has white flowers, to the true species called 'Old English Lavender,' which can grow to 4 ft (1.2 m.). I compromised with *L.a. 'Hidcote'*, which grows to some 2 ft (60 cm.), and bears the traditional blue flowers.

Lavandula angustifolia 'Hidcote'

Santolina chamaecyparissus

Myrtle, *Myrtus communis* will not grow well unless it is given a sunny, warm spot. It seems to be quite at home in my garden planted near the south-west facing wall. The white flowers followed by purple berries make it an attractive border plant, and it has the bonus of aromatic foliage, quite strong when the leaves are crushed.

The 'Cotton Lavender' is, in fact, no relation of the common lavender. It used to be called *Santolina incana*, but the botanists have been playing around again, and have come up with the new name *S. chamaecyparissus*. Not a startling improvement. The grey foliage is very aromatic, though some gardeners do not, I must admit, rate the perfume highly. I like it. The yellow flowers against the grey/green foliage, make it worth its place in any case.

As ground cover, I have used another small shrub, which rapidly increases by means of underground runners. Once established, it will quickly cover a lot of ground, and does a good job as a weed suppressor. The 'Partridge Berry', *Gaultheria procumbens* is sometimes called the 'Checkerberry', presumably by the North Americans from whence it hails. It needs an acid soil, and does best in a shady spot. The small, red fruits have a distinctive aroma when crushed.

Finally, I could not resist two lemon-scented plants. The aroma of lemon in the Lemon Scented Geranium, make up for its less than outstanding flower, while Lemon Thyme has not only a distinctive smell when crushed, but can be used in the kitchen as well.

I think I should offer one cautionary note here. If, as I did, you plant your border rather more densely than you would normally, you must be prepared to spend a little more time on it, and perhaps to forgo some of the annuals when the shrubs and herbaceous plants begin to spread.

I found, for example, that the honeysuckles need constant attention to tying in. They are never happier than when they are scrambling all over other shrubs, who naturally resent their over-friendliness. They grow very fast in the summer, so it is necessary to look at them regularly, and to tie in errant shoots where they belong.

It is also necessary to feed regularly to minimise the effect of competition between the residents of the border, and some trimming back of the more rampant subjects may be needed.

THE HEATHER AND CONIFER BORDER

Some years ago, my old friend Adrian Bloom, came up with a great idea for saving time and labour. Aimed originally at the gardener with little time to attend fully to his garden, he struck on the notion of planting a front garden exclusively with heathers and dwarf conifers. Thus he provided colour and interest literally all the year round, with an absolute minimum of labour. You would certainly not, after the border was established, need to spend more than one hour a week on maintenance.

Now I *like* gardening, and I like to be close enough to my plants to spend more time with them than that. So, I have little interest in labour-saving techniques. But the border looked so stunning, that I found it quite irresistible. In my opinion, there is only one way to treat a really good idea – whatever its source – so I pinched it.

There is another factor about this unique garden that appealed to me. I am an inveterate collector of plants. When I was a kid, I was just as daft about stamps and matchbox tops, and now I find it fascinating to collect as many different species as my garden will hold. My heather and conifer border is a showpiece for my small collection as well as a source of beauty and interest.

In my view, the one and only disadvantage with a complete garden made in this way, is that there is no change. I like to ring the changes and try out different ideas and colour combinations from year to year and that's one of the reasons why I am so keen on mixed borders. But this type of garden is, of course, their

Heathers and conifers
1 *Juniperus media 'Old Gold'*
2 *Microbiota decussata*
3 *Picea pungens 'Globosa'*
4 *Picea abies 'Maxwellii'*
5 *Chamaecyparis lawsoniana 'Minima Glauca'*
6 *Abies balsamea 'Hudsonia'*
7 *Juniperus horizontalis*
8 *Chamaecyparis lawsoniana 'Ellwoodii'*
9 *Chamaecyparis pisifera 'Boulevard'*
10 *Juniperus horizontalis 'Hughes'*
11 *Thuja 'Rheingold'*
12 *Pinus mugo 'Mops'*
13 *Picea pungens 'Prostrata'*
14 *Juniperus procumbens 'Nana'*
15 *Tsuga candensis 'Jeddeloh'*
16 *Juniperus chinensis 'Robusta Green'*
17 *Juniperus communis 'Compressa'*
18 *Juniperus squamata 'Blue Star'*
19 *Erica carnea 'Springwood White'*
20 *Calluna vulgaris 'Beoley Gold'*
21 *Erica cinerea 'C. D. Eason'*
22 *Erica carnea 'Eileen Porter'*
23 *Daboecia cantabrica 'Alba'*
24 *Calluna vulgaris 'H. E. Beale'*
25 *Erica cinerea 'Hookstone White'*
26 *Erica cinerea 'Atrosanguinea Smith's Variety'*
27 *Calluna vulgaris 'Sunset'*
28 *Erica darleyensis 'Arthur Johnson'*
29 *Erica vagans 'Mrs D. F. Maxwell'*

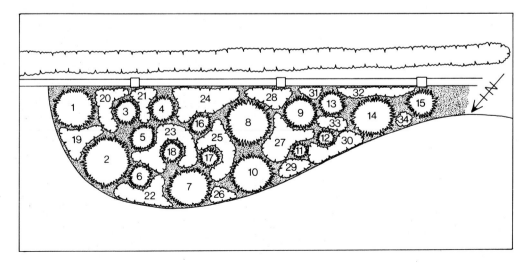

30 *Erica carnea 'Springwood Pink'*
31 *Erica erigena 'W. T. Rackliff'*
32 *Erica carnea 'Foxhollow'*
33 *Erica cinerea 'Foxhollow Mahogany'*
34 *Daboecia cantabrica 'William Buchanan'*

complete antithesis. Consequently, I have devoted a relatively small area to it. Nonetheless, it makes a very pleasing feature.

The preparation of the border should be thorough. While I would agree that the border is labour-saving once it is established, the reverse is the case in the early stages. If there are perennial weeds in the soil, they tend to grow up through the heathers, and can only be removed by hand. It is therefore very important to remove all perennial weeds completely before planting. As I have stated before, the best way to do this is by spraying with a weedkiller containing glyphosate. After spraying, it is worth while leaving the border for a few weeks, allowing any regrowth to appear, and then hitting it with the weedkiller again.

In fact, I must confess, that I learned the value of this advice the hard way. When I planted my border, though I had sprayed a couple of times, the ground was so infested with bindweed that I obviously didn't get at it all. That which was left after planting, multiplied at the speed of light and, however much I hoed and hand weeded, it always reappeared. I was obviously fighting a losing battle. In the end, I decided that sterner measures were called for.

The foliage colours of conifers and heathers can make a striking show all year round

It took me a whole day to paint every leaf of the bindweed with weedkiller, but it was well worth it in the end. There is a glyphosate product available made especially for the job, called Murphy Tumbleweed Gel which is a mixture of the weed-killer plus a viscous liquid that sticks to the leaves. It prevents dangerous run-off onto the leaves of cultivated plants, and holds the weedkiller on the foliage of the weeds long enough for it to be fully absorbed. It works well, but is a bit too expensive for me. So, at the risk of being sued for plagiarism, I modified the idea. Working on the old principle of using soft-soap as a spreader for insecticides, I mixed a little weedkiller with a few squirts of washing-up liquid. Painted on the leaves, it worked like a charm, and my bindweed problem is no more. However, it would be so time-consuming on a big border, that it is well worth while avoiding the problem in the first place by thoroughly spraying before planting.

As with the other borders, it is best to dig thoroughly and work in a generous amount of organic matter before planting.

If you are a collector, planning the border is bound to be a bit haphazard. You will want to collect plants as you see them, and put them in wherever there is sufficient space. Nevertheless, it is worth, if possible, planning at least the conifers before you plant them. Dwarf conifers come in a variety of shapes, sizes, forms and colours, and they can be effectively used in a variety of combinations, one plant setting off the other. Heathers are not quite so critical, though they too demand a certain amount of thought before planting. Here, it is necessary to take into account not only height and spread, but also foliage and flower colour and time of flowering.

If you are going to plant summer-flowering heathers, you must have an acid soil. While the majority of the winter-flowering types will tolerate some lime in the soil, the summer-flowerers will not. If your soil is chalky, and you feel that you *must* have summer-flowering varieties, or if the pH of your soil is so high that even the winter-flowerers will not grow satis-factorily, there are still ways and means of doing it.

Heathers are relatively shallow rooted, so they will grow quite well on chalky soil, if the bed is raised and filled with an acid soil.

Ideally, the border should be raised about 1 ft (30 cm.), en-closing the sides with walling, or with treated timber edging. Then, get hold of some acid soil, and mix it with peat, and a little lime-free grit to provide drainage. The ideal mix would be about the same as John Innes potting compost – 7 parts of soil to 3 parts peat and 2 parts grit.

Some gardeners, I know, rely upon regular doses of seques-tered iron to remedy an alkaline soil. This, in my opinion, is a very expensive and not very effective way of growing acid-lovers. There is no substitute for the right soil, even if you have to buy it in and raise the border.

One of the essentials before planting, is to get to know the eventual spread of the plants. I have underestimated growth in some cases, and have had to move some plants to prevent them spoiling others. One consolation is that they are all fibrous-rooted, and seem to suffer little check to growth, provided they are moved during September or May, and given plenty of water afterwards.

Most heathers and conifers are now grown in pots, so it is possible to plant at any time of the year. Make sure there is plenty of moisture in the soil before planting, and that the pots are watered thoroughly before they are removed. I like to surround the roots of newly-planted subjects, with a few handfuls of moist peat, and to add a handful of bonemeal to the soil before refilling the hole.

The method of planting is described on page 84. There are two great hazards to conifers and heathers immediately after planting. Wind can cause severe browning of the foliage, by evaporating water from the leaves faster than the plant can replace it. Once the foliage turns brown, it will not recover and it will be maimed for life. Avoid this by either erecting a temporary screen of hessian or plastic windbreak material, or by spraying with a transplanting spray. Synchemicals make one called, mysteriously, S.600. It simply coats the foliage with a thin film of transparent plastic, and prevents transpiration. Even having taken these precautions, it is still important to ensure that the plants have plenty of water at the roots, and to spray them over the top from time to time in hot weather.

The second hazard is dogs. If they decide to supplement your feeding programme by their own natural method of foliar feeding, the leaves will go brown and die. It is obviously difficult to protect against dogs, especially if you have one yourself. I'm afraid I have no advice to offer, except to plant your conifers and heathers in a place not easily accessible to our canine friends. Obviously, if you have an open-plan front garden and you plant them there, you are asking for trouble. If you happen to see a dog providing this service, soak the foliage with water as soon as possible after the event, and if you can soak the dog at the same time, so much the better.

Conifers

There are quite a few varieties of conifer sold as 'dwarf' which are not really dwarf at all. Many of these are, in fact, simply slow-growing, and will eventually make quite a big plant. I have seen, on many occasions, *Chamaecyparis lawsoniana 'Ellwoodii'*, offered as a dwarf conifer, and I have also seen them grow to 20 ft (6 m.). If your border is big enough, this may be quite

Early spring colour in the conifer and heather border

acceptable and I have included at least two varieties that will eventually reach this height.

In fact, I started my planting scheme by putting in two fairly tall, upright growers. *Chamaecyparis lawsoniana 'Ellwoodii'* has blue/grey foliage and an upright, columnar habit. It forms the perfect, traditional 'candle-flame' shape in the first few years, though it does tend to open up a bit later. There are several 'sports' or variations of this popular conifer, most of which will not get quite so tall. *C.l. 'Ellwoodii Gold'* is one of the best, with bronzy tips to the branchlets.

My second fairly tall specimen was *Chamaecyparis pisifera 'Boulevard'*. This is a really outstanding, relatively recent introduction. It is rapidly gaining in popularity, and with good reason. The fluffy foliage is a beautiful silvery blue in colour, and is especially intense in the summer. It will eventually grow to something like 10–12 ft (3–3.6 m.), but it is a fairly slow grower.

For absolutely perfect shape in a dwarf conifer, there is nothing to beat *Juniperus communis 'Compressa'*. This one is a true dwarf, growing to only about 3 ft (1 m.), and taking its time to reach that. The tight, dense foliage is a fresh, light green, and it forms a perfect 'candle-flame' shape. It may be a little suspect in its susceptibility to frost damage, but I have had no trouble at Barnsdale, despite several really hard winters.

In contrast to these upright shapes, I have planted several

Chamaecyparis pisifera 'Boulevard'

more bushy, almost round specimens. *Abies balsamea 'Hudsonia'* has deep green, spiky foliage, something resembling the leaves of a yew. It is at its best when it is making new growth in the spring, when the tips of the branches are verdant green. Round and compact, it will grow to no more than about 3 ft (1 m.).

There is such a variation in the shape of dwarf conifers, one can but wonder why, in Nature, this came about. Whatever the reason, the varied shapes can be used to make an interesting effect. Two more ball shapes that are ideal for this type of border are *Chamaecyparis lawsoniana 'Minima Aurea'* and *C.l. 'Minima Glauca'*. Both will grow to about 4 ft (1.2 m.) though very slowly. *'Minima Aurea'* is a bright yellow, while *'Minima Glauca'*, despite the name, which usually indicates a blue colouring, is deep green. Both look very effective when planted in contrast to the taller-growing, upright varieties.

For a complete change in foliage pattern, I planted the beautiful *Chamaecyparis obtusa 'Nana'*. The deep green foliage forms itself into shell-like sprays, the whole, making a flat-topped triangular-shaped bush about 2 ft (60 cm.) high. At certain times of the day, the sunlight catches one side of the bush making intriguing patterns of light and shade.

One of the great advantages of conifers, of course, is that they retain their colour all the year round. In the depths of the winter, when the mixed border is looking a little lifeless, the conifers glow with colour. I particularly like the rich blue foliage of *Abies procera 'Glauca Prostrata'*. This is a prostrate form of the 'Noble Fir', and quite different in habit. Whereas the upright form will grow to a massive tree well over 150 ft (50 m.) tall, this form stays almost prostrate. If shoots do arise from the centre and look as though they want to reach for the sky, they should be cut out. It is well worth the extra trouble. The blue foliage contrasts well with the greens and yellows of the other species, but it is particularly striking in spring when the young growths appear. They are a lighter blue of a quite brilliant, eye-catching shade.

Another blue I wouldn't be without is *Picea pungens 'Prostrata'*. A really bright blue, this one, though again, it may have a tendency to produce upright shoots which should be cut out.

The mat-forming, prostrate conifers must be chosen and planted with care. There are many species that look as though they will simply spread out without growing tall, when they are young, which in fact, when they mature, grow taller and taller. A good example is *Juniperus media pfitzeriana*. As a small plant, it looks ideal for planting in this sort of border. Eventually it will grow to an enormous plant up to about 9 ft (3 m.) high with a spread of 15 ft (5 m.). Definitely not for the small garden.

Much more suitable cultivars are available. *Juniperus horizontalis 'Hughes'* is a relatively new introduction, and, I think, a real winner. It has a neat, symmetrical shape, raising itself slightly above the ground, and the foliage is distinctly silver.

Picea pungens 'Prostrata'

Another superb new one is *Microbiota decussata*. I must confess that I had never heard of the genus at all, until I saw it at the Chelsea Flower Show recently. It grows close to the ground, forming a neat circle of lacy foliage. Bright green in summer, it takes on a rich bronze colour in the winter. Get one if you can.

Before you plant these prostrate conifers, make sure you know their ultimate spread, and plant accordingly. Even then, you must be prepared to adjust. I planted a *Juniperus procumbens* '*Nana*' in my border, and was lax with my enquiries. The Latin word '*Nana*' means dwarf, so I expected the spread to be minimal. I now find that I will have to move several heathers planted near it, which it has completely engulfed. Its ultimate spread, I now discover, is about 12 ft (4 m.). We live and learn.

Finally, two relatively common plants that really deserve their popularity. *Picea glauca* '*Albertiana Conica*' forms a perfect miniature cone. Its foliage is densely packed and bright, apple green in summer. It does have the problem of being very subject to attack by red-spider mite, and may need spraying. Don't let that put you off. It's well worth it.

There are several cultivars of *Pinus mugo*, but two really stand out in my estimation. *P. m.* '*Mops*' forms a dense, round bush of grey-green. It grows to no more than about 1 ft (30 cm.), and is particularly attractive when it is showing its red buds in winter. *P. m.* '*Ophir*' has much the same habit, but its foliage is bright yellow. It looks even better in winter, when the gold colouring seems to adopt a luminous glow.

Pinus mugo

Heathers

There can be no single group of plants that give more value in the garden than heathers, and in that category I include heaths, bell-heathers and lings.

There is, of course, the one restriction of soil. Most heathers require an acid soil, and will not do at all well in chalk. I have already suggested that, if your soil is alkaline, they can be grown successfully in raised beds. An alternative is to stick to those types of heather that are lime tolerant. *Erica carnea* varieties, *E. darleyensis* and *E. erigena* (previously classified as *E. mediterranea*), will all do well in chalky soils. However, I think it is fair to say that even these *prefer* a slightly acid soil, so it will pay to prepare the border by adding a quantity of peat, to use peat when planting, and to mulch around the plants with peat annually.

Heathers are best, in my opinion, planted in drifts of the same variety rather than singly. I plant in threes and fives, though on larger borders, the numbers in the drift can be increased.

I must say, that I have been fairly indiscriminate in my planting plan. Again, my passion for collecting has tempered my 'better judgement'. When I see a new heather that proves irresistible, I buy a few plants and stick them in wherever there is a space. But some rules still apply. Obviously, I plant the taller varieties near the back of the border, or at least where they will not obscure other, dwarfer types. I take into account flower and foliage colour and flowering time. It is possible, with heathers, to have something in flower every day of the year, if the border is big enough. Even if there is not space for them all, the foliage colours are so varied and striking, that the border will glow with colour and interest for twelve months of the year. As it happens, I am lucky to have a slightly acid soil, but even if my garden were on solid chalk, I would find some way of including these beautiful plants.

They are particularly good as a foil to a collection of dwarf conifers. The foliage seems to harmonise with that of the conifers to produce a well-integrated effect.

But, a certain amount of vigilance is necessary. I have found that my heathers are so much at home in my excellent soil, that they grow very fast indeed. If they are allowed to grow into the conifers, they spoil the effect by obscuring the distinctive shapes of the plants, and the overcrowding will eventually cause browning and death of the foliage. So, it may be necessary to trim them back from time to time to prevent competition for light and air. It will do the heathers no harm at all, and if done during July to October will provide a good source of material for cuttings.

There are literally hundreds of varieties of heathers to choose from, and I found it a real headache trying to decide which *not* to grow. If my rich uncle were to die, I'm sure I'd buy fifty acres and grow them all. If I had a rich uncle.

The many varieties of *Calluna vulgaris* are not lime tolerant, but well worth an extra effort if at all possible. They vary in size from about 3 in. (7.5 cm.) to 2 ft (60 cm.) tall. In good soil, some of the more vigorous varieties can grow even taller. Out of the many available, I restricted myself to just half-a-dozen favourites.

One of the best foliage colours in the lings is that of *C.v. 'Beoley Gold'*. The brilliant yellow colouring is retained all year round, and there's a bonus of white flowers in August/September. It grows to a bit over 1 ft (30 cm.) high, and those in my border have spread rapidly.

Somewhat taller growing is *C.v. 'H. E. Beale'* which gives, in my opinion, one of the best displays of flower of them all. The very prolific double pink flowers make a sea of colour from September right through to the end of November.

Obviously, I could not leave out *C.v. 'J. H. Hamilton'*. No relation, of course, though I have been known to lie to my friends! This has been described by no less an authority than *Hilliers' Manual of Trees and Shrubs*, as 'the finest double heather', so I am privileged to share its name. It has a dwarf habit, growing to no more than about 9 in. (23 cm.), so it is ideal for the front of the border. In August and September, it is a mass of the brightest pink flowers.

Earlier in this chapter, I did point out that a border of heathers and conifers gave no opportunity for change. Well, the plants themselves must be permanent, but there is certainly a distinct change of colour with the seasons. One of the best foliage varieties, *C.v. 'Robert Chapman'*, starts in the spring as a brilliant gold. As the year progresses, it changes through yellow, deep bronze and red. All this, and a show of purple flowers in the late summer too. Again, this one will only grow to about 9 in. (23 cm.), so it is another candidate for the front of the border.

Another fine foliage variety that looks well planted in conjunction with the yellows, is *C.v. 'Sunset'*. During spring and summer, it stands out as a splash of bright orange, changing in winter to a deep, reddish-bronze. The flowers are pink in August/September.

Amongst all these pinks and purples, it is good to have a pure white. And a new cultivar *C.v. 'My Dream'*, is one of the best I have seen. The flowers appear in September and last through for a few weeks, eventually turning slightly pink. The dead flower heads are silvery, and they, too, look most attractive for a very long period. It has an upright habit, growing to about 2 ft (60 cm.) and is as tough and hardy as the best.

The 'Irish Bell Heathers' *Daboecia cantabrica* have a charm all of their own. They are perhaps not quite so floriferous as some of the others, but the dainty, bell-shaped flowers remain right through the summer.

I have planted two for a variety of flower colour. *D.c. 'Alba'* is a pure white, the flowers standing out well against fresh green foliage, while *D. c. 'William Buchanan'* is deep crimson.

Both these cultivars, like all Bell Heathers, need a lime-free soil.

The winter flowering heaths, *Erica carnea*, are all lime tolerant, though, as I have suggested, they should still be coddled with plenty of peat, for the very best results. In fact, a mulch of peat around all heathers, apart from improving the soil, provides a dark brown background which sets them off very well.

The great beauty of these heaths, of course, is that they will give a bright display of flowers right through the dark winter months, when there is very little else about. A cheering sight on a grey, winter's day. All grow to about 9 in. (23 cm.).

Perhaps the best known of this group are *E. c. 'Springwood White'* and *E. c. 'Springwood Pink'*. Old varieties, but ones which have never been bettered. They have a vigorous habit, are very free-flowering, right through from January to March, and make excellent ground-cover plants.

Another old variety, *E. c. 'Eileen Porter'* gives real flowering value. Give it a sunny, well-drained position, and it will reward you with deep red flowers right through from October to the following April.

For a bright pink, you can't do better than *E. c. 'Pink Spangles'*. Very floriferous and strong growing, this one will flower from January to March.

For really brilliant yellow foliage right through the year, I have planted *E. c. 'Foxhollow'*. Strong growing and prostrate in habit, this is one of the best yellow foliage heathers I have seen.

Perhaps the widest range of colours comes from the Bell Heathers, *Erica cinerea*. Again, these are lime-haters, so special provisions may have to be made. They flower best if they are given an annual trim over in March, and in fact all heathers benefit from trimming over with shears or secateurs after flowering.

I wish I had room for more, but I have had to restrict myself to just four varieties.

Flowering from June to September, the bright scarlet flowers of *E. c. Atrosanguinea 'Smith's Variety'* is a real joy, despite its enormous mouthful of a name. Planted against the white-flowered *E. c. 'Hookstone White'* it is a certain eye-catcher.

The much deeper, mahogany-red of *E. c. 'Foxhollow Mahogany'* adds a deep richness to the border from July to September, and looks really good planted with *E. c. 'C. D. Eason'*, which has deep pink flowers about the same time.

Erica darleyensis is one of the most useful groups of all. They are all tolerant of a certain amount of lime, flower in the depths of winter, and make excellent ground-cover. The four varieties in my border look well amongst the other winter-flowering heaths.

The longest flowering variety, *E.d. 'Arthur Johnson'*, is tall-growing and vigorous, and is therefore planted near the back of the border. It can grow to 3 ft (90 cm.) high and is covered in rose-pink flowers right through from November to early May. You can't ask for more than that.

I also grow the popular variety *E.d. 'Darley Dale'* for its lighter pink flowers from November to April, and this blends well with the white-flowered *E.d. 'Silberschmeize'*.

A contrast to these lighter colours comes from *E.d. 'J. W. Porter'*, which sports a mass of purple flowers in early spring.

I have included two varieties of *Erica erigena* because they too are tolerant of lime. This group may be more familiar as *E. mediterranea*, but it has also fallen victim to the botanists' reshuffle.

The old variety *E. e. 'W. T. Rackliff'* makes rounded bushes of emerald-green foliage covered in February and March with pure white flowers. *E.e. 'Golden Lady'*, is in fact a sport of W. T. Rackliff, slightly slower growing and with less flower, but boasting brilliant golden foliage.

The Cornish Heath, *Erica vagans* will also tolerate a small amount of lime and contains two well known old varieties that are reliable in producing a striking show of flowers during early autumn. *E.v. 'Lyonesse'* has white flowers, while *E.v. 'Mrs D. F. Maxwell'* flowers at the same time but is a bright rosy pink. Both grow to about 18 in. (45 cm.).

Even a small bed adds colour and interest

THE SCREE GARDEN

To exclude alpines from the garden would mean missing out on an enormous number of plants that have much to offer. But alpines are generally grown, in the garden, in a miniature representation of their natural, mountain environment – a rock garden.

If you have ever been to Wisley, or to many of our great, stately home gardens, you will have seen fine examples of rock gardens at their best. Massive constructions, using hundreds of tons of rock, and providing ideal, almost natural conditions for a collection of alpine plants. But alas, our little plots today, have barely enough room for a decent-sized lawn, let alone a small-scale reproduction of the Alps!

At Barnsdale, the size of the plot put a full-scale rock garden right out of the question but, being a lover of alpines I decided to look around for alternative ways of providing the right conditions, and an equable setting for a small collection. A scree garden seemed like a good alternative.

The Barnsdale scree garden shortly after planting

Scree consists, in Nature, of small pieces of rock, broken off the mountains by the effects of weathering. As the small pieces tumble down the mountainside, they break up further until, when they come to rest at the bottom of the mountain, they vary from pieces the size of an egg, down to gravel and fine sand. Here, certain plants establish naturally, in conditions of very sharp drainage and little in the way of nutrients. They get one really good soaking a year, when they are often covered in snow, and the rest of the year they have to fend for themselves in dry, well-drained conditions, with many of them in full sun.

You would think that very few plants would survive these conditions, and that those that did would be tough and unattractive. In fact, quite the reverse is the case. There are dozens and dozens of species that can thrive there, and many of them would compete happily in a 'flower beauty-contest' with their more pampered cousins.

But, even a full-scale scree garden was beyond the scope of the cottage garden at Barnsdale. So, I decided that, instead of attempting a 'natural-looking' effect which was doomed to failure because of the available room, I would go in completely the

A mature alpine feature

1 Mark out the circle for the bricks using a line and a stick to scratch a mark in the soil

2 After laying the brick circle, dig out the soil to one spade deep

3 Break up the bottom to the depth of the fork and put in a layer of hardcore

4 Cover with a layer of gravel and then replace the soil mixed with peat and grit

opposite direction. What I have created, is a formal area, in a perfect circle. Filled with the appropriate compost and planted with alpines, it looks very well indeed. I sited the area in full sun. Most of the plants I intended to use prefer a sunny spot, and those that like some shade – very much in the minority – could be planted on the north side of the larger plants.

I marked out the circle with a peg tied to a piece of string from another peg in the centre. It is important not to move that centre peg, because it will be needed again to set the bricks.

The edge of the circle was made with engineering bricks, in the same way as described for the edging to the paved area (page 37). The first job was to put in the foundation for the bricks. A circular trench was dug round the perimeter of the circle, and filled with concrete and then the bricks were set as previously described (page 37).

Now came the hard bit. It is essential to provide good drainage, and to fill the planting area with a suitable compost. So, the soil was dug out to a depth of 3 ft (1 m.), and put on one side.

Now, I broke up the bottom of the circle to the depth of the fork. Through my ironstone pan, that was no easy job, believe me. To make sure that the drainage was really effective, I then put in a layer of smallish hardcore. I had plenty of that, left over from digging out the scented border round the paving.

That was covered with a layer of coarse grit, and then I was ready to refill with compost.

It isn't necessary to be quite as accurate in the mixing as one would be with potting compost. I simply measured out in shovelfuls, using two of soil to one of grit and one of peat. The grit I used was fairly coarse – about the size of the shingle used to resurface tar-sprayed roads and drives. It seems rather a lot to use when you're mixing the compost, but that drainage *must* be really good. The circle was then refilled with the compost and allowed to settle for several weeks. In fact, I found that I needed to top it up before starting planting, because it had settled down about 2 in. (5 cm.).

Across the centre of the circle, I set some stepping stones in fairly random fashion. They serve to connect the scree garden with the paved area at the other end of the cottage, but they also have another important function. There are some alpines that prefer a cooler, moister root-run than most, and these could be planted between and at the side of the stepping stones. The soil underneath them would provide just the right conditions.

To set the stones, I simply rammed down the soil, and rested them on a shallow bed of sharp sand. They will not have to take a lot of traffic, so that will be perfectly adequate.

Planting was again, fairly indiscriminate, partly because I have again, collected plants on my travels and planted them wherever there has been room, and partly because the size and shape precludes much pre-planning. The circle is viewed from all round, so there is little need to worry about the variation in height and, since the area is so small, I do not have to worry too much about colour combinations. The whole scree garden can be seen at a glance.

What I did do, was to plant those alpines that prefer a cool root-run, near to the stepping stones, and put those that needed shade, on the sunless side of taller plants. I also made sure that soil conditions were right for the few 'aliens' I used. For example, I have planted a couple of miniature rhododendrons, and these are set in a large pocket of very peaty soil.

To ensure that the drainage round the 'crown' of the plants, where the leaves meet the roots, was well drained and would not hold excess water, I mulched around each plant with gravel after planting. This precaution is most important. Most alpines are fairly hardy, and in fact, I stuck to plants that would not need a lot of coddling during the winter. But the one thing guaranteed to make them suffer, is excess water on the crown. Apart from

that, a mulch of gravel over the whole area reduces weeding and looks very attractive.

I was persuaded to plant a few aromatic-leaved plants like thyme, near to the paving slabs. The idea, I was told, was that, as you walked by and brushed the leaves with your trouser legs, the aroma was released. I have also often read this advice in gardening books. Well, all I can say is, that either my advisers have a much better sense of smell than I have, or very long noses. I could never smell a thing until I got down on my hands and knees! I would reserve the places next to the slabs for the plants that like it cool.

Now, I feel that I should make an explanation for the sake of the purists, about my planting. Alpines are, as their name suggests, plants that naturally grow in a mountainous environment. Some of the plants that I have used do not strictly come within that category. There are several small plants that will thrive in the same conditions but, are not found in natural scree. If they are attractive, I see no reason for omitting them.

1 Bulbs are best planted in groups, setting them in a shallow hole

2 Don't forget to mark their position with canes before re-filling the hole

3 Most alpines are bought in small pots and can be planted with a trowel

4 Water the plants well and re-move them by knocking them out on the trowel handle

5 Set the plants no lower than they were in the pots and firm with your fingers

6 Mulch right up to the base of each plant and over the whole area with coarse grit

To plant every species of alpine plant would require even more room than the fifty acres I dream about for heathers, so once again, I have had to restrict myself. It really goes against the grain. I started by planting a few dwarf shrubs. I avoided, in the main, rockery conifers, for no better reason than that I had already planted my dwarf conifer border, and didn't want to overdo them.

I have always had a soft spot for *Hebes* so I decided to include a couple of dwarf species in the scree garden. *H. pinguifolia carnosula 'Pagei'* is a gem. The only thing cumbersome about this plant is its name! It spreads to form wide mats of grey foliage that look very attractive against the brown of the gravel mulch, and it is covered in dainty white flowers in May. *H. 'Carl Teschner'* grows a little taller, reaching finally about 9 in. (23 cm.). It produces prolific violet flowers with a white throat in June and July.

Berberis thunbergii 'Atropurpurea Nana' forms a dwarf, rounded shrublet, growing slowly to about 2 ft (60 cm.). It does bear small, orange flowers in spring, but its main charm lies in its red/purple foliage which persists, darkening with age, until the winter.

The deep purple foliage of *Berberis thunbergii 'Atropurpurea'*

One of the best shrubs for summer flowers is *Hypericum*. It's a large genus, containing plants growing up to 5 ft (1.5 m.) tall. A little gem for the rock or scree garden is *H. reptans*. I planted this near the edge of the scree garden, where the thin, prostrate stems would overhang and soften the hard edge. It is covered with fat, scarlet buds in late May or June, and these open to large yellow flowers. It is nothing for them to be nearly 2 in. (4.5 cm.) across, and they last well into September or even October.

Another large and varied genus is *Potentilla*. There are a few prostrate varieties that will do well on the rock garden or scree, but none to match *P. frigida*. It forms small mats of foliage, the leaves often taking on a reddish tinge during the summer. Spasmodically throughout the year, it bursts into pale yellow flowers. It may be a bit temperamental about flowering, this one, but if it likes you, it is very rewarding.

There are one or two really dwarf, alpine rhododendrons that make excellent rock or scree garden plants. I have planted two – *R. impeditum*, which grows to only about 8 in. (20 cm.) tall, and is covered with blue, funnel-shaped flowers in April and May, and *R. keleticum*, which has crimson flowers in June.

When it comes to herbaceous alpines, there are literally thousands to choose from, so planning the feature can be quite a headache. The best bet, in my opinion, is to do the job slowly. Visits to nurseries and other gardens will help aquaint you with plants you would like to grow, and it's a fascinating pastime, collecting these tiny plants. Unlike larger herbaceous plants, I feel that these should be planted singly. Many of them, in any case, will spread to form quite large mats.

One of the most eye-catching plants in the herbaceous border is the sulphur-yellow *Achillea*. There are also alpine forms of this valuable plant which will do well in full sun or in shade. *A. clavennae* 'Lewisii' has grey, almost white foliage and sulphur-yellow flowers right from May to September. It grows to about 6 in. (15 cm.).

Another plant with bigger brothers in the herbaceous border is *Allium*. For the scree garden, I chose the dwarf *A. cyaneum* which forms neat, grassy growths of leaf and produces small spikes of bright blue, slightly pendulous flowers from July to September.

Alyssum is a well known annual plant for edging, and has an equally notorious relative in *A. saxatile*, the bright yellow plant that sprawls over walls. Fine for the larger rock garden, but in my limited space, I preferred to plant *A. montanum*. This forms low mounds of grey foliage from which arise sprays of lemon-yellow flowers in June and July.

One of the great charms of alpines is that they have none of the brashness of other, larger-flowered herbaceous plants. To

Armeria maritima

fully appreciate the flowers of many of them, you need to look closely. Just such a plant is *Androsace sarmentosa chumbyi*, whose flowers are just like perfect primroses in miniature. It forms neat mats of woolly foliage, from which the pink flowers arise.

The *Armerias* are always attractive and easy to grow. They form neat green hummocks of foliage from which arise pink or white, almost spherical heads of flower. I particularly like *A. caespitosa* which has flowers of a delicate pink, and *A. maritima* 'Dusseldorf Pride' which is a deep pink, almost red.

Astilbe glaberrima 'Saxosa' is a perfect miniature of the larger species. The deeply cut, green or bronzed foliage is a joy in itself and it also produces neat spires of pale pink flowers in June and July.

The *Asters* are also well known herbaceous plants, and the alpine species are no less attractive. *A. alpinus* has many forms ranging from purple and gold to white. I particularly like *A.a. 'Beechwood'* which has large, solid flowers of blue with a centre disc of bright yellow.

The Bellflowers or *Campanula* are absolutely obligatory. There are many varieties of these beautiful plants and several that are ideal for the rock or scree garden. They are all either white or varying shades of blue, and they are all very prolific in flower. I have planted *C. carpatica 'Bressingham White'*, the light blue *C.c. 'Blue Moonlight'*, and the very deep blue *C.c. 'Oakington Blue'*. All flower from June to August or even longer.

Above: *Campanula carpatica*

Right: *Campanula carpatica 'Bressingham White'*

Campanula portenshlagiana

For something a bit different, try *Carlina acaulis caulescens*. This has rosetted leaves, somewhat resembling an *Acanthus*. From the rosette arise stumpy stems with little, thistle-like flowers. It must have good drainage and a sunny spot, or it may be a little reluctant to flower.

The little low, evergreen mounds of *Draba brunifolia* I find quite fascinating. The foliage is formed into tiny packed rosettes, from which arise minute sprays of bright yellow flowers in April and May.

The prostrate, evergreen mats of *Dryas octopetela* are invaluable in the rock or scree garden. They spread quite rapidly and may have to be cut back a bit if they become invasive, but the wide open flowers of creamy-white make it well worth a bit of trouble.

Leontopodium alpinum

There are several delightful dwarf species of the 'Cranes-bill' family. The foliage is roughly circular in shape and deeply-lobed, making them attractive at all times. I have planted *Geranium argenteum* which has silvery foliage and rose-pink flowers all summer, and *G. cinereum alba* which has greener foliage and white flowers.

'Edelweiss', *Leontopodium alpinum*, is almost too well known to require description. The whole plant is enclosed in dense, white, woolly hairs, and it produces curious, off-white flowers in summer.

The 'Flax' family produces species with flowers of blue, white, yellow and red. They are all free-flowering, and not difficult to grow. One of the best is a hybrid, *Linum* × *Gemmells Hybrid* which grows to no more than about 9 in. (23 cm.) and sports flowers of bright yellow in the summer.

If you have made the compost for the scree garden acid, you will be able to grow what is, in my view, one of the most beautiful of alpine plants: *Lithospermum diffusum* '*Heavenly Blue*', is a prostrate grower with rather rough foliage, producing bright blue flowers from about April to the end of August. Well worth growing if you can.

I am constantly amazed at the immense variation in plants from the same family. The alpine 'Mint', *Mentha requienii*, resembles its larger, herbaceous relatives only in its peppermint smell. It produces tiny green leaves which spread across the surface of the soil like a green film, dotted in summer with minute purple flowers.

There are dozens of varieties of alpine *Phlox* to choose from, all of them easy, reliable and long-lived. They all form close mats of foliage and are all very free-flowering. I particularly like *Phlox douglasi* which is available in many coloured varieties.

Primulas are invaluable in the scree garden, though they prefer a moist soil and a bit of shade. Grow these near the paving slabs, and in the shade of taller plants, for best results. This is a very large genus, so there are literally hundreds to choose from. I planted *P. auricula* '*Blairside Yellow*', which is a charming dwarf species with bright yellow flowers.

Right: *Primula auricula*

Below: *Phlox douglasi*

The *Pulsatillas* are superb alpine plants that no respectable scree garden should be without. I planted the 'Pasque Flower', *P. vulgaris*, which has delightful, ferny foliage and the most superb purple flowers from March to May. There are a few different forms of this variety, in pink, white and red. If you can get it, try also *P. vernalis*, which forms rosettes of leaves from which arise chalice-like flowers of pure white with a central spot of gold. A rare sight indeed.

The genus *Saxifraga* must contain the largest number of alpine plants of all. There are hundreds of different types and varieties, all good in the scree garden. Oh, that one could grow them all. They are generally divided into groups for easier identification.

One of the best of the 'encrusted' saxifrages is *S. aizoon*. They form tiny rosettes of leaves, and there are various different forms giving varying flower colours. I chose *S.a.* '*Rosea*' which has pink flowers during May and June. Like all the encrusted saxifrages, they are worth growing for the foliage alone. Give them the sunniest spot in the scree garden.

The 'Kabschias' also form rosettes of silvery leaves, often pitted with chalk. They are all very free-flowering, and are among the loveliest of the early-flowering alpines. Again, there are many different colours, from which I chose *S. jenkinsiae* for its superb, deep pink cup-shaped flowers.

The 'Mossy' saxifrages make hummocks or mats of tight foliage. They are best grown near the paving slabs, since they relish a moister soil, and they like a bit of shade too. I have *S. 'Cloth of Gold'* which makes golden cushions of foliage and bears white flowers. For a really splendid show of flower, I have also planted the variety '*Triumph*' which makes a spreading mat of blood-red flowers in April until June.

The *Sedums* are another large genus, though many are fairly undistinguished. They are, however, extremely good tempered, growing almost anywhere. Most are spreading by nature and again, there are several flower colours to choose from. They have the distinction of flowering late, when there may not be much else showing colour.

One of my favourites is *S. cauticolum* which forms blue/grey tufts of foliage with large crimson flowers in late summer. Perhaps even better is *S. spathulifolium* '*Capablanca*' which has grey, almost white foliage and charming yellow flowers.

The Houseleeks, or *Sempervivums* are also very numerous and they deserve a place for their foliage alone. All form large rosettes almost like cacti, and there are several different flower colours. I have been unable to resist collecting many different varieties, but my favourite still, is the 'Cobweb' houseleek, *S. arachnoideum*. This makes small, tightly packed rosettes with the tips of the leaves joined by fine hairs. They look just as though a spider has made his web over them'. As an added bonus, they produce what

Right: *Saxifraga 'Cloth of Gold'*
Below right: *Sedum cauticolum*

I think are the best flowers of the genus that I have seen. Bright, rose red, and borne in great profusion.

Of the thymes, I have planted both the creeping types and the upright. There are many varieties available in each. I like *Thymus serpyllum 'Coccineus'* which forms creeping mats of thread-like branches, and is covered in red flowers in June and July. But for a real splash of colour all the year round, I don't think you can beat the bush-forming *T. citriodorus*, the Lemon-scented Thyme. It makes a really bright little bush of pure gold, about 9 in. (23 cm.) high.

Iris danfordiae

Violas are delightful flowers anywhere, and the alpine species are particularly good in the scree garden, provided they can be given a little shade. The easiest, I think, may be *V. cocculata*. I grow the variety 'Freckles', which has plenty of white flowers, liberally speckled with blue.

Bulbs add a great deal to the scree garden. They are easy to grow, and can generally be left in the ground to come up year after year. I grow about half-a-dozen different kinds, and I'm adding to them every year.

Any dwarf, spring-flowering bulbs can be used. I particularly like the tiny species narcissi like *Narcissus minimus* which bears tiny yellow flowers in February, on stems no more than 3 in. (7.5 cm.) high.

There are several varieties of *Iris* which will flower from as early as January, through to March, making a fine show of colour at a bleak time. *I. bakeriana* is lavender blue and sweetly scented. *I. danfordiae* is worth growing for its lemon-yellow flowers, while *I. histriodes major* is deep blue.

Anemone blanda

I wouldn't be without the cheering sight of *Anemone blanda* around March. The bright blue, daisy-like flowers make a vivid show, and there are pink, mauve and white forms too.

The lovely little *Puschkinia libanotica* is well worth a place for its silvery blue flowers, made bolder by deep blue stripes. I must say though, that I found that one rather hard to come by, so it may need searching out.

THE WILD GARDEN

While most gardeners spend half their time getting rid of weeds, I have been actively encouraging them at Barnsdale. Of course, many weeds like couch grass, ground elder and annual thistle, simply have to go. They are so invasive that they could quickly take over the whole garden. But there are some species of 'weeds' that are a positive asset in the garden.

Over the past thirty years or so, I have watched with horror, as many of our native wild-flowers have been destroyed to the point of extinction by modern methods of agriculture, new building projects and road systems and by the local council's obsession with 'tidying up' roadside verges by constant mowing. I rarely see a wild violet these days, and it is years since I have noticed a cowslip locally.

The Nature Conservancy Council mixture of wild flowers and grasses

What is worse, is that this wholesale destruction of our native plants, has a dramatic effect on the other forms of wildlife. Without their familiar host plants, birds and butterflies will disappear, and bees and other insects will have nowhere to feed. For me, one of the great joys of the garden is the sound of insects and birds on a hot summer day, and the occasional glimpse of a butterfly fluttering from plant to plant.

I don't want to get into a long, philosophical discussion about the whys and wherefores, but, what I was determined to do was, in a small way, to provide an alternative home for a few of our native plants. At the same time, I would encourage birds, insects and who knows, perhaps the odd small mammal.

I am lucky to have a little copse at one side of the garden and the ideal method of marrying it in with the cultivated part was an area of native grasses and wild-flowers between the two. But I have seen much smaller areas used to provide a home for a few wild plants and grasses, and there is no doubt that it is very effective in introducing a wider range of butterflies and other insects into the garden.

Though the country garden is more amenable to this sort of scheme, I have seen a very successful wild area in a garden right in the heart of London. Even there, butterflies and bees choked their way through the exhaust fumes to this wildlife oasis.

Of course, the idea of 'wild' gardening is a far cry from our normal methods, and produces a very different result. One would need to be more of a naturalist than a gardener to devote the whole garden to it. Yet a small area within the garden is a delight.

For the very busy gardener, it would be a godsend. After the initial establishment, there is nothing more to do, except to cut it twice a year. The reward is an area of waving grasses, studded with a great variety of multicoloured wild-flowers and buzzing with the activity of insects. A few trees and shrubs, planted here and there, provide cover and food for birds and small mammals.

The Nature Conservancy Council, ever mindful of the need to provide alternative habitats for wildlife, have produced a wild-flower/grass seed recipe, ideal for the purpose. The seed mixture in now available from specialist seedsmen. There are basically two mixtures, one tall and the other short, though of course, there is no reason why you should not add your own favourites, provided they are likely to succeed in your area. The ones most likely to do well are, of course, those that grow or have grown locally in the wild. You may need to search your memory, or take advice from a long-term local resident.

The mixtures contain more than a dozen native grasses, and up to twice that number of different species of wild-flower. I just can't resist names like, 'Lady's Bedstraw', 'Spiny Restharrow', 'Rough Hawkbit', and 'Sweet Vernal-grass' – they're so much more romantic than the logical Latin.

Left: Honeysuckle is almost certain to attract a myriad butterflies

The first thing to do when preparing an area for this sort of mixture, is to get rid of existing weeds. This may seem, at first sight, to be a bit of a paradox. On the one hand you are killing weeds, while on the other, you are, immediately afterwards, sowing them again. Because, after all, wild-flowers are only what we gardeners call weeds.

The point is that, apart from all the problems wild-flowers have to face from Man, they also have to fight a lot of competition from their own kind. Particularly where land has been in cultivation, the more rampant species are likely to get well established and to completely smother the less vigorous competition. Bear in mind too, that you will almost certainly be introducing plants that will be expected to flourish in conditions where they perhaps wouldn't in the wild. Many of our most beautiful wild-flowers grow in places where the more rampant species are not at home, so they may need a certain amount of coddling.

What seems even more illogical, is to suggest ridding the area of weeds with a herbicide – the very reason why many of our wild-flowers are becoming rare. Nevertheless, that is certainly the best way to ensure a weed-free seed-bed.

I sprayed with glyphosate, cultivated, and then sprayed again when some of the weeds had regrown. Remember that it is important to allow at least ten days after spraying, before cultivating, to allow the weedkiller to get down to the roots.

The preparation of the seed-bed, is exactly as for sowing a normal lawn. Cultivate first, consolidate by treading all over with your weight on your heels, and rake to a fine, firm tilth.

No fertiliser should be used with this seed mixture. Even here, there will be competition amongst the plants, and in very fertile soil, the more rampant will have an unfair advantage. What we are aiming for, is an exact replica of conditions in the wild, so normal, unfertilised soil is to be preferred.

Before sowing the seed, it is important to mix it thoroughly. There is a great disparity in the size of the seeds, since there are so many species included. Unmixed, the smaller seeds will sink to the bottom, and the result will be a patchy distribution. To be on the safe side, the seed can be mixed with about twenty times its volume of sharp sand before sowing.

The sowing rate can be much lower than that recommended for lawn seed. Many of the grasses and wild-flowers have much smaller seeds than normal lawn grasses, so there are very many more in an ounce. Good results will be obtained from sowing at $\frac{1}{4}$ oz per sq.yd (7 gm per sq.m.).

After sowing, rake the seed into the surface, and protect the area from birds.

If you are starting a new garden, or the soil has not been cultivated for some time, it is likely that the fertility will be low.

In that case, the rate of growth of the new seedlings is likely to be slow. Indeed, some of the wild-flowers will not germinate at all for several months, and this leaves the area open to another infestation by unwanted weeds. To avoid this, the newly-sown plants should be protected by a 'nurse crop'.

This is simply a vigorous grass, which will quickly colonise the area providing an effective cover and preventing invasion by weed seeds. Once the wild-flowers and grasses have germinated and started growing, however, it is necessary to get rid of the nurse crop. The problem is solved by a fiendishly cunning trick.

The nurse crop used is an *annual* rye-grass called 'Westerwolds Ryegrass'. It should be incorporated in the mixture using about half the amount of rye-grass seed by weight. It will grow very vigorously in the first year after sowing, but, provided it is prevented from seeding, it will automatically die out at the end of the year, leaving the area free from competition, for the wild-flowers.

Obviously, the rye-grass will provide its own competition in the first year, so growth must be controlled to give the other species a chance. This is done by mowing and, in the first year, it *must* be done at the right time. Failure to do so could mean that the rye-grass will set seed and will therefore be present in greater strength next year. It will also provide some of the less vigorous wild-flowers with too much competition, and they will die out.

The first cut should be done about six to eight weeks after sowing, depending upon the amount of growth the nurse crop and any unwanted weeds have made. Ideally, cut with a rotary mower down to about 3–4 in. (7.5–10 cm.). This will effectively reduce competition from the rye-grass and weeds, and may kill off some weeds completely. The cut grass should be raked off and put on the compost heap.

During the remainder of the year, cut at two-monthly intervals until October.

In the second and subsequent years, maintenance will be much less, and there will be something to show for your efforts too. The wild-flowers will have all germinated and should, in the absence of too much competition, be growing strongly.

Two cuts only will be necessary. The first is made in April, cutting down to about 2 in. (5 cm.). Then, all you have to do is to sit back and wait for a fine show of tall, waving grasses and a multicoloured show of flowers, from May to October. The second cut is made in October, by which time the grasses and wild-flowers will have set seed for the following year.

Throughout the years, the flowering population of the wild garden varies. Some plants will be more vigorous in one year, only to be overtaken again by another species the next. Thus, the display of colour will vary from year to year, and so will the species of insects and birds visiting the plants.

Attracting wildlife

Strangely, it is considerably more difficult to get hold of wild trees, shrubs and herbaceous plants, than it is to buy cultivated species, unless you grow them from seed. Of course, many can be found growing in the countryside, but I would most certainly *not* recommend that they should be dug up and transplanted to the garden. There is rarely much chance that they will survive, so that sort of desecration of the countryside is futile. They will be much better left alone.

But after all, cultivated plants, with a very few exceptions, are simply 'improvements' on wild species, and there are many that will do as good a job of attracting wildlife to the garden. Since I planted a few bird, bee and butterfly attractors, I am sure that their visits to my garden have increased.

All these plants are attractive garden plants as well, so they can be included in the mixed border to good effect.

Most berried trees and shrubs will provide food for birds in the winter. I know that many gardeners will complain that they prefer to keep their attractive berries, but I must say that I derive great pleasure watching my winter visitors eating Christmas lunch. Bear in mind, that if you keep them happy and they become regular customers, they will dine on aphids and all sorts of garden 'nasties' in the summer. Most varieties of *Cotoneaster* will produce enough berries for you and the birds as well, while *Pyracantha* is even better. I have also planted a few flowering Crabs which have proved a great attraction. *Malus 'Golden Hornet'* and *M. 'Evereste'* are superb flowering trees, which attract the bees as well in the spring and incidentally, make excellent pollinators for apples.

The 'Snowberries' are also much sought after by birds. The best for the wild garden is *Symphoricarpus laevigatus* which will form dense thickets of growth, providing good cover for birds. It is one of the species favoured by country gamekeepers for pheasant cover.

Elders are excellent native small trees and shrubs. Their flowers attract bees and other insects by the million, and their black, edible berries are a favourite with birds. Unless your garden is very big, the 'Common Elder', *Sambucus nigra* is a bit too rampant, and tends to sucker and seed all over the place. Better for the small garden, though not quite so attractive to wildlife, is *S. racemosa 'Plumosa Aurea'*, the 'Golden Cut-leaf Elder'. It makes a much smaller shrub, and its golden foliage, white flowers and red berries make it an attractive plant for the border.

The 'Mountain Ash' family are well known for their masses of red berries in autumn, both by gardeners and by birds. I have planted *Sorbus Aucuparia 'Sheerwater Seedling'*, which has quite spectacular orange-red berries.

Bees will visit most flowering plants, but there are several

Right: *Malus 'Golden Hornet'*
Below: *Symphoricarpus laevigatus*

which seem to prove irresistable. Don't worry, by the way, about getting stung by the bees you have been kind enough to invite into your garden. They are generally much too busy to take any notice of you, and will only attack a human in cases of extreme danger. Leave them alone, and they'll happily get on with their work. They are, of course, essential for producing a good crop of fruit and, if you collect your own seed from garden plants, they will help there also.

Many of the flowering cherries are especially attractive to bees early in the year. Superb flowering plants, they are a necessary requirement of every garden.

One of the best for the wild garden is *Prunus avium*, the 'Mazzard' or 'Wild Cherry'. In April, it is covered with delightful, single, white flowers that attract bees like a magnet. An added attraction is the rich autumn foliage colour.

Prunus avium

Of the Japanese cherries, one of the best is *P. serrulata 'Tai-Haku'* which forms an imposing, flat-headed tree of great architectural value even when leafless. In spring, large pink buds open to masses of pure white, pendulous flowers. Again, the rich autumn colouring is an added bonus.

Our native Lime, *Tillia euchlora*, is a well-known attractor of bees, but a bit large for most gardens. Silver birch, *Betula pendula*, is by no means too large, and will add that natural woodland effect to the wild garden. I have planted both the common form and *B. utilis*, the 'Himalayan Birch', which has attractive, coppery-brown, peeling bark. Both produce quantities of pollen much loved by bees.

Many shrubs attract bees, so in the main, I have planted those which will also provide good cover for birds. The barberries are particularly useful, and I don't think there are better varieties for the purpose, than *Berberis stenophylla* and *B. darwinii*. Both produce yellow flowers in April/May, and both are evergreen.

Buddleia davidii serves the double purpose of attracting bees and droves of butterflies. There are several different flower colours, from white, through reds and pink to deep purple, all of them good. For the best display of flowers, these are best pruned back hard in February.

Buddleia davidii

Above: *Sedum spectabile*
Left: *Syringa vulgaris*
Right: *Acer palmatum 'Atropurpurean*

A most useful plant in the wild garden, is the Lilac. These carry a heady perfume to attract bees, butterflies and a host of other insects, and they also provide good cover for birds. For the wild garden, one of the varieties of *Syringa vulgaris* would be most suitable.

There is, to me, a great joy in attracting butterflies to the garden. There is no more beautiful insect, and they must have romantic connotations for us all. They seem to be having a tough time of it in the wild these days, because alas, many are suffering from farmers' improved and very much increased spray programmes. If we are not to lose them altogether, it is essential to provide them with another habitat in the garden.

As I have mentioned, *Buddleia* and *Syringa* are two of the best attractors, and the Lavender in the scented garden pulls in quite a few. But, I suppose the plant that has proved most successful for me, is the herbaceous *Sedum spectabile* sometimes known as the 'Ice Plant'. I have planted two varieties, *S. s.* '*Brilliant*', which produces flat heads of pink flowers in late summer, and *S. s.* '*Autumn Joy*', which has darker flowers and green foliage that turns brownish-purple in autumn. A most attractive plant.

Of course, there are many species of wild-flowers and what would otherwise be obnoxious weeds, that will attract bees and butterflies too. Amongst them, for example, is the common Stinging Nettle. Perhaps not the plant that everyone would like in the garden, but it is a fact that a diversity of planting increases the numbers of different species that will visit the garden. So, I try to leave just a few of these not-so-attractive plants, just for the sake of the wildlife. Well, that's my excuse, anyway.

TREES

With much of the garden planted with shrubs, herbaceous plants and alpines, and the lawns well established, it began to look 'lived in'. What it lacked, very noticeably, was height. However well the lower level is furnished, a garden needs that third dimension that can only come from trees.

At Barnsdale, I had to be careful about what I planted, and where I planted it. Most small gardens are the same, but often for different reasons.

It must be realised right from the start, that trees take up more room than any other plant in the garden. They tend to cut out light, and they can cause problems of excessive dryness. They take a fair amount of nutriment from the soil, and they can even cause structural damage to nearby buildings. None of these problems is insoluble, provided care is taken in choosing the right subjects. How often have we all seen the misguided gardener plant the ubiquitous weeping willow in a small front garden? A beautiful plant to be sure, but it must be realised that the skinny sapling bought from the garden centre, will, one day, grow into a fifty-foot giant, with a spread that covers the whole garden.

Small gardens need small trees, and there are plenty of first-rate varieties to choose from.

At Barnsdale, I had a further problem. It was imperative that I did not obscure the views of the countryside beyond, and yet I needed tree cover to prevent the ravages of the wind. So, my trees had to be hardy in the main, and judiciously sited to leave space between to take in the views.

The worst of the wind comes across the valley from the south-west where there is nothing to break its force. Of course, there are cold winds from the north and the east, but there is a certain amount of cover from those sides. My first job then, was to choose a selection of trees that would give some shelter to the garden, would not grow too tall and at the same time would be decorative enough to give the added height that the garden so obviously needed. Once they were established, other, more tender species could be planted.

The area to be planted was some way away from the house and on the other side from the drains. Near the house, it's important to avoid the really strong-growing trees like sycamores, poplars and willows. They have a very strong root system that can damage drains, push up concrete, and even affect the foundations of the house. On heavy clay soils, hungry trees can be even more of a problem. They tend to extract water at such a rate, that the clay actually shrinks, leaving spaces under the foundations, which could lead to sinkage and subsequent cracking. Such trees should be planted at least forty feet away from buildings.

The first choice that sprang to mind for the exposed south-eastern side, were the *Acers*. A large and varied genus, which includes many highly decorative trees and shrubs, some of them far too tender to plant in such a situation. But two species are very hardy indeed. *Acer pseudoplatanus* is our near-native Sycamore. It was, in fact introduced from Europe, but has become so much at home here, that it is now regarded as a 'naturalised Briton'. There are many distinct and very beautiful varieties. The one I chose was *A. p. 'Simon-Louis Freres'*. In spring, the young leaves are variegated green, cream and purple. A really stunning sight. They do tend to become greener later in the year, but retain their colour well past midsummer.

The 'Norway Maple', *Acer platanoides* is no less hardy and contains some beautiful foliage varieties. I planted two of these to form a triangle with the *A. pseudoplatanus*. *A. p.* '*Crimson King*', is one of the most striking of the species. It makes a large, round-headed tree with big leaves of deep, crimson-purple, right through the season. It makes an excellent companion for *A. p.* '*Drummondii*'. This variety has variegated leaves of green, margined with white. When the sun shines through these two, they almost glow with colour. '*Drummondii*', does have one drawback. It has a tendency to revert back to its original green foliage. If any branches arise that show leaves that have reverted, they should be cut right out as soon as they are seen.

Acer pseudoplatanus 'Drummondii'

Cotoneaster watereri

A bit nearer the house, I wanted something not quite as vigorous as the *Acers*, but still as hardy. I chose one of the few small, evergreen trees available – *Cotoneaster watereri*. This is a vigorous little tree with long, glossy green leaves, white flowers in the spring, followed by masses of red berries in autumn. It is, in fact, classified as 'semi-evergreen', but even in hard winters and on my exposed site, my one has retained its leaves all winter.

To add contrast in form, I set this off with a fine specimen of the 'Kilmarnock Willow', *Salix caprea* '*Pendula*'. Now this one can be a bit confusing. There are two 'clones' or forms of this tree, one male and the other female. Nurserymen and even botanists appear to have been at odds about which was which for years, though they now seem to have sorted it out. The male is the 'Kilmarnock Willow', and the female form is known as 'Weeping Sally'. Both make small trees, nothing like the size of the well known 'Weeping Willow' *Salix vittelina* '*Pendula*', and eminently suitable for small gardens. The male form has thicker, more widely-spaced branches, and carries big, yellow, 'pussy willow' catkins in spring. The branches weep right down to the ground, and the catkins appear long before the leaves, making it a very eye-catching sight. The female form has thinner, more closely packed branches, and the catkins are white. At the risk of being accused of chauvinism, I must say, that the male form is, in my opinion, vastly superior.

Salix caprea 'Pendula'

I picked up a useful tip about these and other weeping trees, when I bought this one from my very experienced, local nurseryman. Very often, weeping trees tend to grow their branches down one side of the stem only, making a somewhat unbalanced tree. If you buy one like this, face the bare side away from the prevailing wind. That will slow up the growth on the windward side, and speed up the leeward branches, so that the tree will eventually develop into a perfect umbrella shape. I did, and it works.

That solved the wind problem on the south-east side of the garden. Now I needed a couple of trees on the south side, and again I had to think carefully. Here, was one of my best views, which I simply had to retain, yet this part of the garden was crying out for added height. I decided to 'frame' the view between two trees so that I could still see between them and underneath the branches. What I needed were two trees with stiffly upright branches that would grow into a sort of inverted triangle.

There are a couple of perfect candidates for the job, both beautiful trees and easily available at almost any nursery or garden centre.

Japanese flowering cherries are, perhaps, the most popular flowering trees seen in modern gardens, and with good reason. There can be few trees that offer such a breathtaking sight in early spring, when they are ablaze with enormous garlands of pink, or white flowers. One of the most widely planted is *Prunus* '*Kanzan*'. It is a vigorous tree whose branches ascend stiffly in just the form I wanted. It does tend to open out a bit at the top as it gets older, but would still leave plenty of room for my 'peep-hole' underneath. It is one of the most showy of all trees in April, when it is covered with large, double, deep pink flowers. The young foliage is an attractive coppery colour, turning to green in summer and later to an attractive orange/yellow in the autumn.

About fifteen feet away, I planted my other upright grower, *Laburnum watereri* '*Vossii*'. This is undoubtedly the best laburnum for growing in gardens. It makes a relatively small tree, with steeply ascending branches, and attractively lobed leaves. The long, pendulous garlands of yellow flowers are borne in profusion in May and June. One word of warning. All parts of this plant are poisonous, and particularly the seeds. This variety is, in fact, the least poisonous of the laburnums, and little Johnny would have to eat half a hundredweight to do him any real harm, I expect. Still, if you have young children who make a habit of eating almost anything, it is perhaps better avoided.

Prunus 'Kanzan'

Laburnum watereri 'Vossii'

I have already mentioned the two varieties of 'Silver Birch' I planted in the wild garden. Near to those, I also planted a 'Weeping Birch' in order to make the transition between cultivated and wild garden a little more gradual. Not everyone would agree, I'm sure, but I felt that the somewhat 'brasher' garden plants seemed to somehow 'fight' the more subtle, less showy natives, and that something between the two would help bridge the gap and keep the peace.

There are a few varieties of weeping birch, but by far the easiest to come by, and in my view the best, is *Betula pendula 'Youngii'*, 'Young's Weeping Birch'. It forms a small, mushroom-headed weeping tree that droops right down to the ground. The bark is the characteristic silver, and the graceful branches make it attractive even in winter when it has lost its leaves.

Now that I had some protection from the wind, I could afford to plant some less hardy trees. In my view, one of the most beautiful of small, foliage trees is the golden-leaved *Robinia pseudoacacia 'Frisia'*. There can surely be no tree that makes a brighter splash of yellow than this one. It has beautifully shaped, 'acacia' foliage that holds its bright colour right through from spring to autumn. I planted it in the border near to the shrub, *Cotinus coggygria 'Royal Purple'*, where it makes a superb contrast to the almost purple foliage. The one and only drawback with

Betula pendula 'Youngii'

this tree, is that it tends to suffer from 'die-back' in the early stages. To minimise the problem, buy it in a container.

One of the delights of spring for me, is the foliage of the Whitebeam, *Sorbus aria 'Lutescens'*. I say it's a luxury, because the foliage colour lasts little more than a month, when it fades to a relatively dull green. It has another slight 'rush of blood to the head' in the autumn, when it bears not very conspicuous bunches of red berries, and the foliage turns a russet/gold colour. But the bright, silvery-white leaves are an outstanding sight in early spring, and a sure sign of better things to come after the winter. If you can only grow one or two trees in your garden, perhaps this is not the one, but I wouldn't be without it.

Above: *Malus floribunda*

Left: *Robinia pseudoacacia* '*Frisia*'

Right: *Sorbus aria* '*Lutescens*'

For an early show of flower, there can be few trees to equal the flowering crabs. One of the earliest and best, is *Malus flori-bunda*, the 'Japanese Crab'. It carries its deep pink buds at the same time as the white open flowers, making a quite spectacular, multicoloured show. There is a second display of colour in late summer from bunches of smallish, red, cherry-like crab-apples. An excellent flowering tree for a small garden.

One coniferous tree that has long impressed me is the 'Blue Cedar', *Cedrus atlantica* '*Glauca*'. Now this is not a small tree and should not be considered a possibility for a small garden. It is fairly slow-growing, but will eventually reach massive propor-tions. If you have the room, however, it makes a superb specimen. Its branches are somewhat pendulous, and its needle-like foliage is the brightest blue of any conifer I know.

Finally, of course, we mustn't forget the fruit trees. Because I have a small plantation on the trial-ground at Barnsdale, I decided against planting free-standing apple, pear or plum trees in the cottage garden. They do make excellent decorative trees though, with their bright show of blossom in the spring and the colourful display of fruit in late summer. But, with a south-facing wall, who could resist a fan-trained peach? It makes a cheering sight in the spring when it's in blossom, and when I eventually pick my own, home-grown peaches, it will be well worth the extra trouble of training. I have used the variety 'Rochester' which fruits in August and has a particularly fine flavour.

On the same wall, I am also growing a fan-trained Quince. This too, has very pretty pink/white flowers in spring, and will eventually produce large, yellow fruits that are both decorative and useful. The flesh is rather bitter, but makes excellent quince jelly and is a fine addition to home-made wines to add a bit of extra 'bite'. I have planted the variety 'Vranja', which produces, early in its life, fruits of exceptional flavour.

Planting

Trees, like shrubs and herbaceous plants, can be bought either bare-rooted or in containers. The same rules apply. Bare-rooted plants can only be lifted and replanted in the dormant season between November and March, and the earlier they can be planted within that time, the better. If they can be got in during early November, when there is still some warmth in the soil, they will stand a good chance of making some root and getting established before the real winter weather sets in.

Container-grown plants have the advantage that they can be planted at any time of the year, provided the weather and soil conditions are favourable. It is never a good idea to plant either bare-rooted, or container-grown plants when there is frost in the ground.

Personally, I prefer to buy trees that have been field-grown and are lifted during the autumn, rather than those grown in containers. With few exceptions, they transplant very well, and they tend to be sturdier and better shaped when grown in the field without the root-restriction imposed by a pot.

Nowadays, many trees are sold as 'feathered' specimens. This means that they remain unpruned, with branches all the way up the stem. This is done partly, I suspect, to save the labour of pruning, and partly because those side branches help to thicken up the stem in the early stages. They can, of course, be grown on in this way, but I like to see trees with a bare stem and a well shaped head on top. The best bet, if you buy feathered trees, is to leave the 'feathers' on for the first couple of years, and then to prune them right back, to leave a bare stem. Select well placed branches to form the head, and cut out any that are crossing, or growing towards the centre of the tree. Most ornamental trees require little pruning after that.

If bare-rooted trees arrive at a time when it is impossible to plant them immediately, they should be 'heeled-in' as described on page 84, or left in their bundles in a cool, frost-free shed. They require a little more attention than shrubs, because all trees, whatever the size, will need to be staked and securely tied.

It is generally recommended that stakes should be driven at least 2 ft (60 cm.) into the ground, and should be long enough to reach to the top of the stem, just below the lowest branch. There is, however, a new school of thought that suggests that much shorter stakes are just as effective. The argument is, that the stake is used to prevent rocking of the tree at the roots, but that it is better to allow the stem to move in the wind. This way, there is less strain on the stake, and it is likely to remain more solidly in the soil. I have tried both methods under my very windy conditions, and now lean towards the latter argument. Certainly the tops of the trees move considerably, but the roots

Careful planting of young trees will always pay dividends

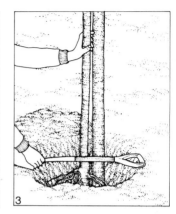

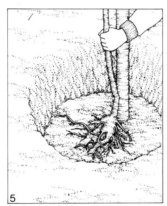

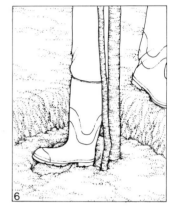

remain firmly in the soil, and there appears to be no permanent bending of the stem. However, my one reservation would be where there is a constant wind in one direction. This, I feel, could lead to permanent bending of the stem, and a lop-sided tree would result. Under these conditions, I would recommend staking the tree with two strong stakes with a cross-bar between.

Whichever way it is done, it is important that the stake should be thicker and stronger than the tree. It sounds obvious I know, but a tour of garden centres produced only one which stocked stakes anywhere near strong enough for trees. I am lucky to have a wood-yard nearby where I can buy 'rustic' poles about $2\frac{1}{2}$ in. (6.5 cm.) in diameter. I strip the bark from the bottom, point them and soak them in Green Cuprinol for a few days before use.

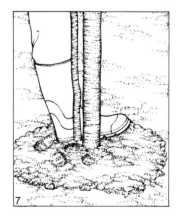

It is also essential to use a proper tie. There are several excellent plastic tree-ties available, though they are a bit expensive. I cut strips of green polythene from compost bags, double them over and tie them fairly loosely. I then make a collar by winding

1 Dig a hole large enough to take the full root-spread, and break up the bottom

2 Bang the stake in before planting to avoid damage to the roots

3 Make sure that the tree is set at the same level it grew on the nursery

4 Cut off damaged roots and spread out the root system evenly in the hole

5 Cover with a little soil and shake the tree up and down to work soil between the roots

6 Half fill the hole with soil and firm it round the roots with your boot

7 After completely refilling the hole, firm the soil again around the roots

another strip of polythene round the tie between the post and the tree to prevent chafing. Whatever you do, *don't* use nylon string or wire. Both will eventually cut through the bark of the tree causing severe damage and probably complete loss of the tree.

Before planting bare-rooted trees, inspect the roots for damage. Any cracked or broken roots should be trimmed back with a pair of sharp secateurs.

Dig a hole large enough to take the full spread of the roots without having to bend them back on themselves, and then bang in the stake to the required depth, before setting the tree in the bottom of the hole. If the tree has been 'bottom-grafted', as many are, you will be able to recognise the grafting point by a pronounced bulge in the stem. The tree must be planted so that this is well above ground. Otherwise, plant them at the same level they grew on the nursery, as will be clear by the soil-mark on the stem.

If your soil is heavy, or particularly poor, it is a good idea to mix some peat in with the soil you have dug out, before refilling. If the soil is good, there is no need for any additions except a couple of handfuls of bonemeal, sprinkled on the heap.

Put a little soil over the roots, and shake the tree up and down, to work it down between the roots. Then half fill the hole and tread the soil down firmly with your boot. Refill the hole completely, and re-tread, making sure that the soil is really firm. The tree can then be tied to the stake, using two ties, one at the top and one halfway down the stem. I like to put a small nail in the tie to fix it to the stake, just to prevent it slipping down.

Container-grown trees are planted in just the same way as shrubs (page 83), except, of course, that they too must be staked Again, the stake should be driven in before planting to avoid possible root damage.

From time to time, it is wise to inspect the tree-ties to make sure they haven't worked loose. It will also be necessary to loosen them a little as the tree grows, to prevent constriction.

TUBS, TROUGHS AND BASKETS

Gardens, for me, are all about plants. Attractive and useful though they may be, I almost resent the areas of paving I have had to put in, because they prevent me from planting. Or do they?

I have, as I mentioned, softened the paved area with planting in special holes left during the construction, and in the spaces between the slabs. This still leaves an area of grey, that needs livening-up. I've done it by planting in tubs and troughs, strategically placed for maximum effect and convenience. The walls of the cottage, and my little woodshed have been decorated with hanging baskets, and window-boxes overflow with colour most of the year. There's a lot you can do with containers.

Containers

Go into any garden centre, and you'll find all sorts of containers made from every conceivable type of material from plastic to pottery, from concrete to cast-iron. All will grow plants satisfactorily, and the choice must depend upon personal taste and your particular garden. In an older cottage, like mine for example, plastic would look completely out of place. I chose some attractive terracotta tubs, and those made from reconstituted natural stone. They are not cheap, by any means, so I had to collect mine over a long period. Others I made myself.

One container that I'm particularly proud of, was made from an old kitchen sink that had been thrown out to make way for a clinical-looking stainless-steel thing. The old sink was made from glazed china, so it had to be disguised to look like stone. I got the recipe from an old gardening book, so I thought I'd give it a try: surprise, surprise, it worked.

Sink gardens are attractive miniature landscapes, especially useful in the small garden

Above: Geraniums and petunias make a brilliant display

Right: a terracotta container planted with geraniums, *helichrysum* and *artemisia*

Above: wooden barrels cut in half make ideal tubs

Right: brightening up an otherwise dull corner

167

The first job is to cover the old sink completely with a bonding material. I used one called 'Uni-bond', but I believe there are others. Your builder's merchant will be able to advise. When the bonding was nearly dry, I mixed up a revolting-looking mess made from equal parts of sharp sand, cement and sieved peat. It's important to make the mixture fairly dry, or it keeps slipping off. It's just as well to keep a bit of the mixture to one side, just in case you make the consistency too runny.

The 'mortar' is then spread over the container in a layer about $\frac{1}{4}-\frac{1}{2}$ in. (6–13 mm.) thick. Cover the whole of the sink, inside and out. The covering won't be seen inside, of course, but it makes a more hospitable surface for plant roots.

This first layer will be a bit patchy and uneven – mine was, however hard I tried – but it made a good base for the second layer. Don't worry about making too good a job of levelling the second coat. It looks a lot more like stone if it's left a bit rough. To add to the illusion, I stippled the surface with a stiff brush and then allowed it to dry for several days. It really does look very much like an old stone trough, and cost a fraction of the price of the real McCoy.

The sink, of course, had a hole in the bottom, so, when I set it up on the paving, I sloped it very slightly to ensure that the water drained towards the hole.

Wooden window-boxes are quite easy to make, I used 6 in. × 1 in. (15 cm. × 2.5 cm.) planed softwood for the sides and bottom, and a couple of pieces of 8 in. × 1 in. (20 cm. × 2.5 cm.) for the two ends. The fixing blocks in the corners of the box were made from $1\frac{1}{2}$ in. × $1\frac{1}{2}$ in. (4 cm. × 4 cm.) timber. Don't forget to drill plenty of holes in the bottom for drainage.

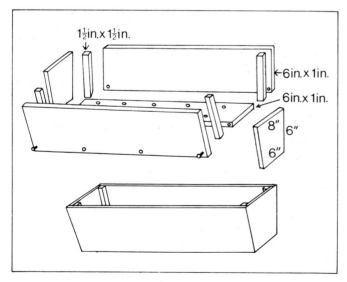

A windowbox can be easily made from a few lengths of timber

I must confess to being entirely prejudiced about hanging baskets. There are several plastic models around these days which are not, I feel, a patch on the good, old-fashioned wire ones. They are too small to be able to make a decent show, and it's impossible to plant through the sides as you can with a wire basket. The essence of a good hanging basket, is that it should eventually become a ball of flower. It has to be viewed mainly from the bottom, so the garish colours of plastic are, to my mind, to be assiduously avoided.

Filling

It is absolutely essential that containers should be well drained. Some concrete containers I have bought, had holes about the size of a pencil in the bottom, which were quite inadequate. I solved the problem by enlarging the hole with a hammer and cold-chisel, so that it was at least the diameter of a broom-handle. Some plastic tubs are designed for use inside as well as out, so they have no holes in the bottom at all. For use outside, they must be drilled. It is a simple job, either with an ordinary wood-drill, or with a red-hot poker.

The holes in the bottom have two functions. Firstly, they allow the free passage of water through the tub, and secondly, they allow air to circulate through the compost. To ensure that this is possible, I like to set the tubs on a couple of slates, so that they are raised very slightly off the ground. Some tubs have holes in the sides as well, making this unnecessary.

The bottom holes must be covered to prevent blockage by soil. In the old days of clay pots, this was no problem. There was always a bit of broken pot kicking around that would do the job admirably. Now, it may be necessary to cover the hole with a small piece of slate, supported on one side by a stone, to allow air and water to pass through freely. Then fill the bottom couple of inches with some coarse drainage material. Small stones or gravel would be ideal.

It must always be remembered that container-growing is a very artificial method of growing plants. So, while ordinary garden soil may be fine in the borders, it will not do at all for containers. Good compost is essential. It must be free draining, though capable of retaining water and nutrients.

The best medium is John Innes potting compost. Soil-less composts are fine, provided you can guarantee that you will never forget to water them, and that you will be around every day to give them the attention they require. The problem is that peat-based composts tend to dry out much faster than those made with soil. And, once they dry out, they are extremely difficult to wet again. This is particularly so with hanging baskets.

The soil in John Innes composts acts as a buffer against drying out, while the peat and sand provide good drainage and water-holding.

I use J.I.P. No. 3, though the only difference in the potting composts is the fertiliser content, and this will have to be supplemented at a later stage in any case.

Planting

Tubs and troughs can be planted with annuals for a maximum show of colour, or with permanent plants if desired. Window-boxes and hanging baskets are generally planted with annuals.

If the containers are to be permanently planted, it is imperative to choose plants that will thrive under the restricted conditions. We have all seen those tired looking conifers languishing in pots much too small for them. Far from being a cheering sight, they look rather sad. But tubs and troughs, and particularly sinks, planted with alpines are different again. These are plants, as we have already seen, that require little in the way of nutrients, and need only a very restricted root-run. So, they are tailor-made for containers.

The permutations for planting a sink-garden are endless. I have seen some quite fascinating little miniature landscapes made in this way, using dwarf conifers, like *Juniperus communis* '*Compressa*' and *Juniperus squamata* '*Pygmaea*', together with a selection of low-growing alpine plants. They do extremely well, and need very little attention. For alpines, it is wise to make the compost a little freer draining than J.I. compost, and I would suggest adding about one third coarse grit.

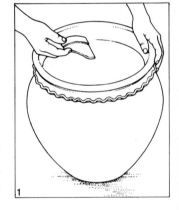

But, for a really dramatic show of colour, there are no plants like the annuals. With careful planning, the tubs and troughs can be ablaze with colour from early spring, right through to the first frosts of winter.

Start the year by planting half-hardy annuals in late May or early June. There is a vast amount of choice, almost any half-hardy annual being suitable, provided it is not too tall.

I like to start by planting something really dramatic in the middle of the tub, or at intervals towards the back of window-boxes. Geraniums are ideal, since they will go on flowering all the season provided the dead flowers are removed regularly. Fuschsias are also excellent, and they come in a variety of colour combinations to add great variety.

In front of the centre plant go the slightly shorter annuals like petunias, salvias, tuberous begonias etc. They too, will flower right up until they are cut down by the autumn frosts.

Right at the front of the container, are planted short edging annuals like alyssum and lobelia, and a selection of trailing plants to hang down over the front of the container.

Trailing varieties of geraniums and pendulous fuchsias make a good show, and trailing lobelia is a sure winner.

1 Before filling with compost, put a layer of drainage material in the bottom of the tub

2 Ideally, use a soil-based compost like John Innes, to avoid excessive drying out

3 Plant one tall subject in the centre, and fill round with lower growing plants

4 Finish off the planting with trailing plants set round the edge

5 Give the tub a good watering to settle the compost around the plant roots

When planting, the plants can be fairly crammed into the containers. They won't mind being planted very closely together, and they will fill the container with flowers that much quicker. After planting, give them a good watering, and then check them every so often to ensure that they don't dry out. Remember that pots and window-boxes will dry out much faster than plants in the open ground, and they may need water, even during wet weather. This is particularly so with window-boxes which may be protected from the rain by the overhang of the eaves.

During the season, it may or may not be necessary to feed. Probably, in the first season after filling the containers with compost, there will be enough fertiliser to make extra feeding unnecessary. In the second season, unless fertiliser is added at planting time, it will almost certainly be necessary.

Annuals will, in fact, flower better if they are starved, but they won't grow as well. So, the art is to try to produce large plants, and then to stop feeding to induce plenty of flower.

Once the winter frosts come, the annuals will blacken and die. It is best if you can anticipate the first hard frost and remove the geraniums and fuchsias, since they can be propagated from cuttings to provide plants for the following year.

The annuals can then be removed, the containers cleaned up, and left for the winter.

There are two ways of coping with the spring display. If you can bring yourself to remove the summer plants a bit early, say in September, they can be planted with spring-flowering bulbs and biennials. If the show during September is too good to remove, the plants for the spring display will have to be grown on in pots or boxes. I prefer the latter method, because I hate taking out plants that may have a month or six weeks of service left in them.

Most spring bulbs can be used in containers, though it is wise to avoid the taller growing tulips unless your garden is very sheltered. Without support, they tend to flop over in the slightest wind, and can look very untidy. I use daffodils and narcissi, short botanical tulips, grape hyacinths, crocus, snowdrops and hyacinths.

For a really full tub of colour, some bulbs, like daffodils and narcissi, can be planted in layers. Put a layer of compost in the bottom of the container, and set the bulbs on it so that they are almost touching. Then cover them with more compost and set another layer in the same way. The bottom layer will push through the bulbs above them and really fill the pot.

Alternatively, the containers can be planted with biennials raised from a late spring sowing outside. I always reserve a small patch in the vegetable garden for raising plants like wallflowers, *cheiranthus* and forget-me-nots for filling my containers. In fact, the best show of all probably comes from a mixture of biennials and spring bulbs.

The alternative is to raise all these plants in pots, ready for transplanting as soon as the summer show is over. Biennials can be grown on happily in an open frame, while bulbs can be set in boxes of peat and covered up in a corner of the garden, with ashes or peat. When they are removed, they can be transplanted to the containers in early spring.

1 Line the inside of the basket with sphagnum moss. Alternatively use a piece of plastic sheet

2 Fill to halfway with a soil based compost, again to avoid excessive drying

3 Place a tall plant, like a fuchsia or geranium in the centre of the basket

4 Fill round with smaller plants and trailing subjects round the edges

5 Push trailing plants through the moss from below

6 If the basket is lined with polythene sheet, small holes will have to be cut

7 Hang the basket in the greenhouse for a couple of weeks before putting it out

Hanging baskets

Hanging baskets make a ball of living colour which really livens up otherwise bare walls. I hang them all round my patio, as high as I can reach with the watering can. That way they bring the vividness of colour that only annuals can provide, to another level in the garden. Being so easily transported, they can be planted up early and brought on in the greenhouse, so that, in late May when the danger of frost is past, they are already in full bloom.

The wire baskets are best lined with moss, which is generally available at the florist. However, I always line mine with green polythene cut from a compost bag. It's cheaper, and the fast growing annuals soon cover it up.

When the basket is lined with moss or polythene and filled with compost, I like to set it on top of a large flowerpot on the greenhouse staging for planting up. That way, it will stay rock-solid.

Planting the top, is much the same as planting a tub. Start in the centre with a geranium, or a fuchsia or something similar, surround it with lower growing annuals and finally put trailing plants around the edge.

Then hang the basket on a hook from the roof of the greenhouse, to plant the outside of the basket. If you have lined it with moss, the plants can simply be pushed through it after

pushing the moss to one side. If it is lined with polythene, it will be necessary to cut small cross slits in the polythene. For the outside planting, I use several colours of trailing lobelia, or sometimes other trailing plants like the variegated *Tradescantia* which can easily be grown from cuttings.

When planting is finished, give the baskets a good soaking with water to settle the compost round the roots and leave the baskets in the greenhouse until the end of May or the first week in June.

INDEX

Numbers in italics refer to illustrations

THE GARDENERS' WORLD COTTAGE GARDEN

PICTURE CREDITS
The publishers would like to thank the following for the use of their photographs on the pages listed. Geoff Hamilton: pages 7, 12, 15, 69, 76, 87, 130, 163, 166. Harry Smith Horticultural Photographic Collection: pages 25, 26, 27, 33, 34, 41, 42, 51, 52 (Top), 54, 55, 57 (Above), 58, 74, 75, 77, 79, 90, 91, 94, 95 (Right), 99 (Top left), 100 (Left), 101 (Above), 104 (Above), 109, 111, 112, 114 (Top left), 115, 117, 119, 122, 123, 125, 131, 137, 138 (Top left), 139 (Below), 141, 142 (Below), 144, 146, 148, 151, 152, 153, 156, 158 (Top), 160, 161 (Above), 167 (Below & below right). Michael Warren AIIP: pages 49, 52 (Below), 53, 56, 57 (Right), 93, 95 (Below right), 97, 98, 99 (Right), 100 (Below), 101 (Above top and right), 102, 104 (Left), 105, 106, 110, 113, 114 (Below), 116, 124, 129, 135, 138 (Below), 139 (Right), 142 (Top), 149, 150, 155, 157, 158 (Left), 159, 161 (Right), 167 (Above top and above right). T. C. E. Wells, 143.